In This Issue

PIVOT MAGAZINE

Founder
Jason Miller

President
Juddene Villarin

Web Master
Joel Phillips

Designs
ReliableStaffSolutions.com

Copyright © 2025 PIVOT

ISBN: 978-1-957217-93-2

Contact
Jason Miller
Founder
1151 Eagle Drive #345
Loveland, CO 80537
jason@strategicadvisorboard.com

Shelby Jo Long
Editor-in-Chief
shelby@strategicadvisorboard.com
877-944-0944

From the Editor

Growth That Actually Makes Sense

We built this issue for founders and leaders who are done chasing growth that looks good on paper but drains in practice.

There's a shift happening. People are stepping back to reassess what really moves the needle and what just burns resources. Whether it's crafting smarter landing pages, rethinking how you launch, or finally getting serious about client acquisition, this month's content is built for clarity and results.

You'll find a strong focus on working smarter from remote productivity to data-driven marketing to personalized financial planning. The common thread is strategy over scramble. Alignment over ego. Substance over scale.

If you're ready to stop following the crowd and start building something that actually fits, you're in the right place.

Shelby Jo Long
Editor-in-Chief

From the Desk
Of The President

The Growth Myth Is Wearing Thin

September invites a different pace. A chance to breathe, reflect, and rethink the noise that's been driving so many decisions.

This issue challenges the obsession with chasing scale for scale's sake. More leaders are realizing that growth without direction is just expensive chaos. What matters more is building a business that actually works for your life, your values, and your vision.

Inside, you'll find tools to help you do just that. Whether you're refining your launch, optimizing your marketing, managing risk, or building a remote team that performs. This issue delivers the clarity needed to make smart, sustainable moves.

You don't need to keep up with everyone else. You need to align with what works.

So as you reset for the months ahead, ask yourself:

- What are you still chasing that no longer serves your mission
- Where is your energy producing real traction
- What would happen if you stopped scaling and started simplifying

Let us build with precision. Let us lead with purpose. Let us grow on our own terms.

JUDDENE VILLARIN *J.V.*

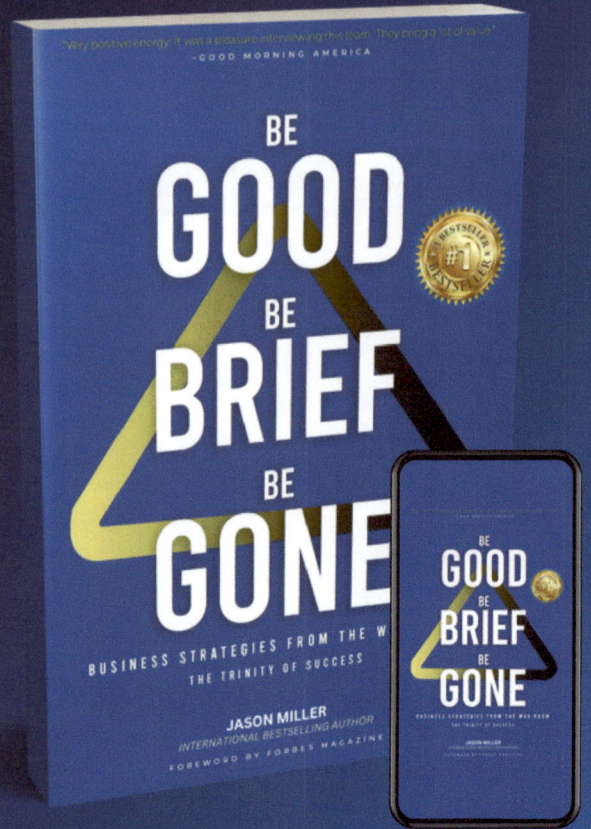
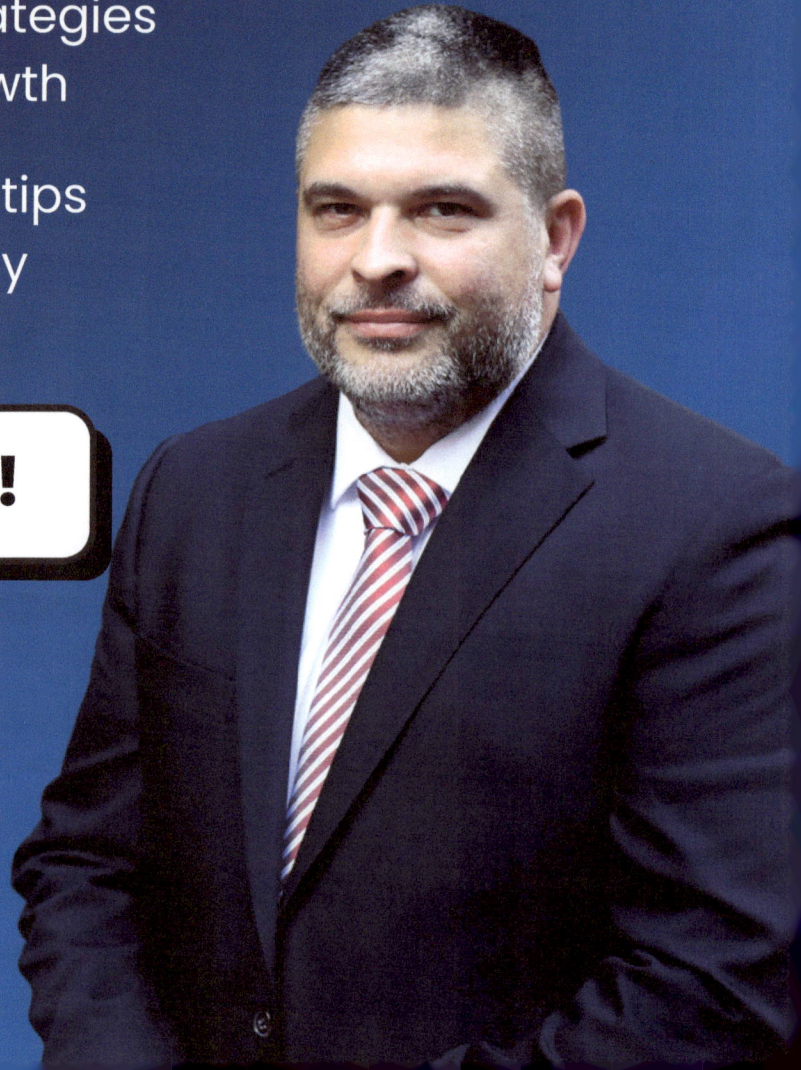

Scale Is a Lie

Why Founders Are Walking Away from Big Growth

Scale doesn't always mean success. Sometimes it just means more stress.

Once, scale was everything. The startup mantra was simple: build fast, raise faster, and chase exponential growth at all costs. But that era is losing its grip. A quiet, intentional rebellion is unfolding across the business landscape. More founders are questioning the true cost of rapid scale - burnout, blurred vision, and businesses that feel more like runaway trains than purposeful ventures.

Today, success is being redefined. It's no longer about inflated valuations or massive teams. It's about control over your time, clarity in your mission, and the calm that comes from building sustainably. This shift isn't just about rejecting venture capital. It's about rejecting the myth that bigger is always better.

From solo operators to lean teams, a new generation of entrepreneurs is rewriting the rules. They're choosing impact over impressions, long-term value over short-term hype, and alignment over hustle. In doing so, they're showing that there's power and freedom in growing on your own terms.

The Myth of Scale

For decades, scale was seen as the ultimate marker of success. Entrepreneurs were taught to pursue it relentlessly - raise more capital, hire faster, expand aggressively, and dominate markets. Books, startup accelerators, and investors all echoed the same message: growth at any cost equals winning. But the aftermath has painted a more sobering picture. Burnout among founders and teams. Internal chaos and culture cracks. Mass layoffs following inflated valuations. And flashy exits that, while impressive on paper, leave founders feeling disconnected or disillusioned.

The truth? Growth isn't inherently bad. In fact, it's necessary. But blind scaling, scaling without purpose, profit, or long-term vision, is a recipe for instability. It often leads to founders spending more time pitching than building, managing bloated teams instead of honing their craft, and chasing headlines rather than lasting value.

Sustainable growth means knowing when to say no, staying grounded in your purpose, and scaling with intention not ego.

Founders Who Opted Out

Meet the founders who chose a different path.

- A SaaS entrepreneur who capped their team at 10 and hit $3M in profit.

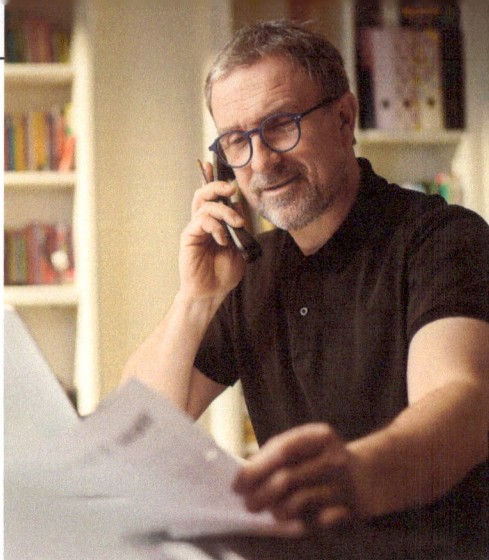

- A retail brand owner who turned down acquisition offers to preserve their company's soul.

- A media founder who scaled back from 30 employees to 5 and is happier, healthier, and more profitable.

Their stories show that stepping back from the scale race doesn't mean giving up. It means building something that actually lasts.

The Cost of Chasing Scale

It's not just about money. The cost of hypergrowth often includes:

- Burnout at the founder level

- Culture collapse inside teams

- Product drift, where purpose is lost in pursuit of revenue

- Personal relationships sacrificed for the grind

And the kicker? Many scale-obsessed startups never even

make it. The runway ends. The investors get spooked. The dream gets diluted.

The Freedom of Staying Small

Smaller companies often hold a powerful advantage: agility. Without layers of bureaucracy or investor pressure, they can move faster, pivot smarter, and stay deeply connected to the people they serve. That proximity to the customer builds trust, loyalty, and insight that large organizations struggle to replicate. There's also a unique freedom in saying no. No to bad-fit clients who drain your energy, no to investors who don't share your values, and no to growth strategies that overcomplicate what was once simple and joyful.

When founders shift their focus from building a business to sell, to building a business to live in, everything changes. Decisions become clearer. Priorities realign. The pressure to perform for optics fades, and what's left is something more meaningful: a business that fits your life, not the other way around.

Founder Insight: "I used to chase numbers to feel valid. Now I chase peace, purpose, and profit. It's enough."

Redefining Success

Success isn't scale. It's staying in love with your work.

It's owning your time. Leading with intention. Building something you never want to escape from.

In the era of burnout, economic uncertainty, and AI churn, this isn't just a trend. It's a survival strategy.

The founders who will thrive in the next decade won't be the ones with the biggest teams. They'll be the ones with the clearest reasons.

Choose wisely. Growth is optional. Freedom is not.

Best Practices for Crafting High-Converting Landing Pages for SEM

In today's fast-paced digital economy, search engine marketing (SEM) is an indispensable tool for businesses aiming to drive traffic, generate leads, and boost conversions. A key component of SEM is crafting ads that attract clicks, but the journey doesn't end there. Once users click on your ad, the real challenge of converting that interest into action begins.

A landing page is the destination that users are directed to after clicking on an ad. Unlike a homepage that offers general information about a business, a landing page focuses on a single offer or call-to-action. But for a landing page to increase conversion rates, it must provide an experience that aligns with the promise made in your ad.

Given the influence of landing pages in your overall SEM efforts, you need to ensure you craft well-optimized ones. In the following sections, we'll explore the best practices for creating SEM landing pages that maximize conversions and help businesses succeed in Singapore's competitive digital marketplace through effective pay-per-click marketing tactics.

Ensure Your Message Matches the Ad

As mentioned previously, consistency between your ad and landing page is crucial for maintaining user trust and interest. When users click on an ad, they expect to see a landing page that delivers on the promises made in the ad copy. If there's a disconnect such as offering a 10% discount in the ad but not mentioning it on the landing page - users are likely to leave. This leads to high bounce rates and wasted ad spend.

To ensure message alignment, carry over the same language, visuals, and offers from your ad to the landing page. This means that if your SEM ad promotes "Free Next-Day Delivery Across Singapore," for instance, your landing page should

prominently feature this benefit in the headline.

It's also beneficial to include the same keywords in both the ad and landing page copy, which not only improves user experience but also contributes to a higher quality score in platforms like Google Ads. A higher quality score can reduce cost-per-click (CPC) and improve ad placement.

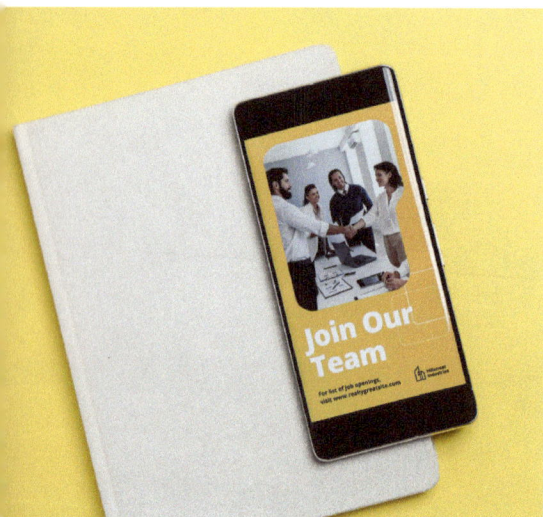

Moreover, strong message match fosters credibility. When users see that the landing page reflects the expectations set in the ad, they're more likely to trust the brand and take the desired action whether that's making a purchase, signing up for a newsletter, or requesting more information.

Another effective tactic is to personalize the landing page experience using dynamic text replacement. This method adapts content based on the specific search terms or ad variants that led the user to the page, creating a more tailored and relevant experience.

Craft Clear and Compelling Copy

Your landing page copy plays a pivotal role in persuading visitors to take action. It should be concise yet powerful, informative yet persuasive. The goal is to quickly convey your value proposition while addressing potential objections that users may have.

Start with a bold, benefit-driven headline that immediately captures attention and communicates the value of your offer. The headline should be clear, specific, and action-oriented. Follow it with a compelling subheading that provides supporting information and encourages users to continue reading.

Use bullet points to highlight key features and benefits, making the content scannable and easy to digest. Ensure the copy speaks directly to the target audience by addressing their needs, pain points, and desired outcomes.

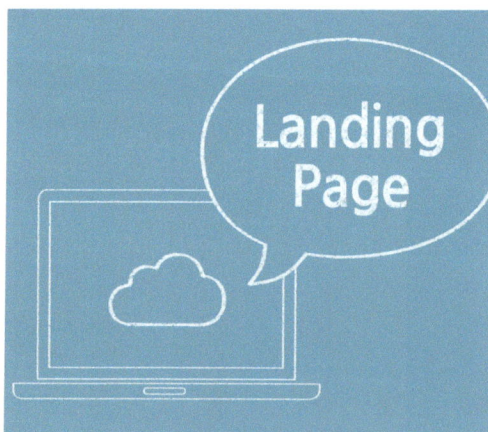

Avoid jargon and keep the language simple and relatable.

Incorporate psychological triggers such as scarcity ("Limited-time offer"), urgency ("Act now"), and social proof ("Trusted by over 10,000 customers") to motivate users to act quickly.

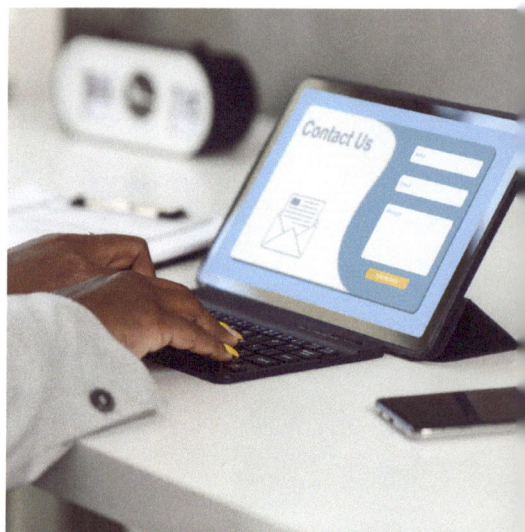

Remember that clarity beats cleverness. While creative copy can be engaging, it should never come at the expense of clarity. Users should instantly understand what the offer is, why it matters to them, and what action they should take.

Add Engaging Visuals

It's also best to add visual elements on your landing page, but be sure that they complement your copy and enhance its overall appeal. Opt for high-quality images, videos, and infographics that help capture attention and make your offer more persuasive.

For example, showcasing professional photos of your product, an explainer video, or before-and-after images can add credibility and visual interest. Videos can also increase engagement and time-on-page, which are positive signals for user experience and SEO.

Interactive elements such as sliders, animations, or hover effects can further enrich the visual experience, but be cautious not to overuse them. Excessive animation can distract from the main call-to-action or slow down the page.

Ensure all visuals are optimized for fast loading and responsive across all devices. Compressed images and mobile-friendly design are essential to avoid slow load times, which can negatively impact bounce rates and conversions.

Use visuals strategically to guide users' attention. For example, images of people looking toward the call-to-action button can subtly direct the viewer's gaze and increase clicks. Color psychology can also be leveraged to evoke the right emotional responses—for instance, using green to indicate safety or blue to promote trust.

Remove Any Distractions

A cluttered landing page can confuse visitors and dilute the impact of your primary message. To keep visitors focused, ensure your design is clean and distraction-free. Eliminate unnecessary navigation bars, pop-ups, or links that divert attention from your call-to-action (CTA).

Center the design around a single, clear goal. If the objective of your SEM campaign is to get visitors to sign up for a service, the landing page should guide them directly to the sign-up form without unnecessary detours.

Avoid including competing offers or secondary CTAs that may confuse users. Everything on the page should support the main goal and make the conversion process as frictionless as possible.

Utilize white space to create a sense of openness and improve readability. This not only makes the content easier to scan but also directs attention to key elements such as the headline, value proposition, and CTA.

Perform regular audits to identify and remove elements that don't contribute to the user journey. Even small changes, like reducing the number of form fields or eliminating auto-playing videos, can have a significant impact on conversion rates.

aren't necessary to the sign-up.

Use progress indicators for multi-step forms to reassure users and show them how much more they need to complete. Autofill options, mobile-optimized keyboards, and accessible error messages can further enhance the user experience.

Test your forms regularly to identify usability issues and fix them promptly. Conduct A/B tests to compare different versions and optimize for higher completion rates.
Provide clear, concise instructions and use trust signals such as data privacy assurances to reassure users about submitting their information.

Ultimately, the goal is to make the conversion process as smooth and effortless as possible. Every additional step or hesitation point is an opportunity for the user to abandon the page—so eliminate barriers wherever you can.

Avoid Conversion Friction

Another strategy when crafting high-converting landing pages is to avoid conversion friction. This refers to any obstacle that makes it difficult for users to complete the desired action. Lengthy forms, confusing layouts, or unclear instructions can frustrate users and lead to drop-offs.

To reduce friction, streamline the process by asking for only essential information. If you're capturing leads, stick to basics like name, email, and phone number instead of requiring other extensive details that

Build Trust and Credibility

In general, consumers tend to be cautious buyers by placing a high value on trust and reliability. To build credibility on your landing page, include trust signals that reassure visitors of your legitimacy.

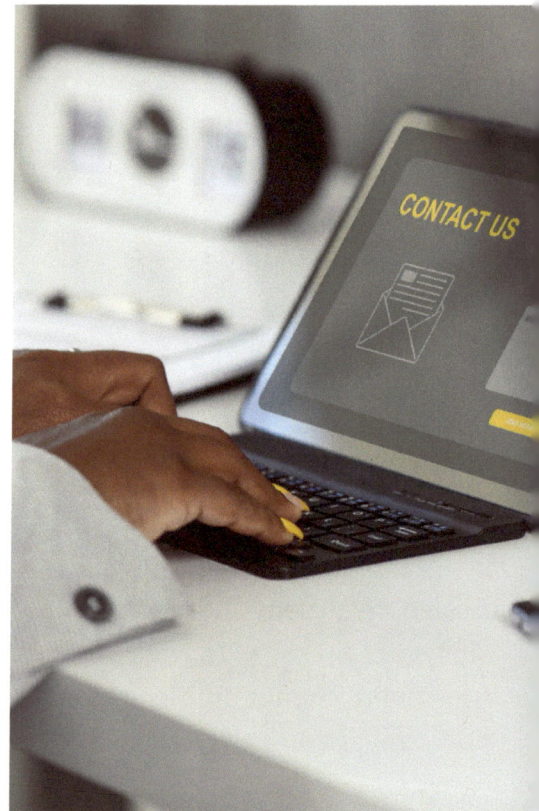

One example is customer testimonials, preferably from local clients. These can create a sense of relatability and trust, as they offer reliable social proof that potential customers can connect with. Testimonials featuring names, photos, or even short videos are especially powerful.

Displaying badges for secure payment methods, certifications, or industry awards can further enhance credibility. If your

business has partnerships with recognized local organizations or brands, highlight these associations prominently as well.

Include real-time statistics, case studies, or user-generated content (UGC) to show that your offering delivers tangible results. Even something as simple as a "Featured In" media logo strip can reinforce authority.

Ensure transparency around pricing, guarantees, and return policies. When users feel that you're being upfront, they're more likely to complete the desired action and trust your brand for future purchases.

A professional and consistent design across all your digital assets—ads, landing pages, and follow-up emails—also contributes to trust. An amateur or inconsistent look can raise doubts, even if your product or service is legitimate.

Optimize the Landing Page for All Devices

With Singapore having one of the highest mobile penetration rates in the world, optimizing your landing page for all devices is non-negotiable. Responsive design ensures that your content adjusts seamlessly to different screen sizes, providing an optimal experience whether users are browsing on a desktop, tablet, or mobile phone.

In addition to responsive design, prioritize fast loading times. A slow page can frustrate users and cause them to abandon the site before it even loads. Place key elements like CTAs and forms in easily accessible locations, such as at the top of the page, to make navigation effortless for mobile users.

Use larger fonts, tappable buttons, and simple layouts to ensure that your landing page remains easy to use on smaller screens. Conduct device-specific testing to identify any layout or functionality issues.

Google rewards mobile-friendly pages with higher quality scores, which can improve ad performance and reduce costs. So beyond user experience, mobile optimization also supports your SEM campaign's overall effectiveness.

Monitor mobile-specific metrics, such as bounce rate and average session duration, to ensure your mobile experience is as engaging as the desktop version. Continuously test and iterate based on user behavior across devices.

RSS>
Reliable Staff Solutions

Guiding Growth: Alvie Jakosalem

on Building Trust & Balance in Business Formation

"Working at RSS has taught me how much you can grow when you're surrounded by the right people and the right support"

When did you join the RSS team, and what brought you here?

I joined the RSS team in 2022. I was drawn to the opportunity to grow professionally while helping businesses move forward.

What's your favorite part of working at RSS?

I really value the work-life balance here, and I appreciate being aligned with clients I genuinely like working with.

How has your role evolved since you started?

I began with basic client support but over time, developed into a trusted guide for licensing, with stronger insight into client needs and more complex problem-solving responsibilities.

Describe your typical workday or work-from-home setup

My day includes assisting clients via email and phone, attending team meetings, and balancing deep work with collaboration to keep things productive and engaging.

If you could describe RSS in three words, what would they be?

Collaborative, innovative, empowering

STAFF STATS

- 🎧 **Work Anthem:** Noah Kahan, Norah Jones, or a solid jazz playlist

- 🍪 **Favorite Snack:** Matcha and oatmeal cookies

- 💡 **Fun Fact:** Loves solo dates, random adventures, and karaoke hangouts

"

To me, being reliable means showing up and doing your part, being the person others trust without hesitation.

Maximize Your SEM Conversions with Strategic Landing Page Design

A well-crafted landing page is essential for turning SEM clicks into conversions. Consider implementing the best practices mentioned above and regularly monitor performance metrics to identify areas for improvement. With a strategic approach and continuous optimization, your SEM landing pages can drive meaningful results in Singapore's competitive digital landscape.

Whether you're promoting a new product, capturing leads, or encouraging sign-ups, the landing page is where conversions happen. Make every click count by delivering a seamless, engaging, and conversion-optimized experience.

The Power of Networking: Building Strong Business Relationships in a Connected World

Networking remains one of the most vital components of career advancement and business success. In an increasingly digital world defined by remote collaboration and hybrid work models, building meaningful professional relationships can open doors that résumés and cover letters often cannot. In fact, studies show that approximately 85% of job opportunities are secured through networking, highlighting the immense value of connecting with the right people at the right time.

Yet despite its significance, many professionals still find networking intimidating or confusing. Some feel awkward initiating conversations, while others struggle to identify where or how to begin. Add to that the shift toward virtual interactions, and the process can feel even more complex.

However, successful networking today is no longer about handing out business cards at events. It's about cultivating authentic, mutually beneficial

relationships. Whether through LinkedIn messages, virtual coffee chats, or in-person meetups, the aim is to create lasting professional value, not transactional encounters.

We'll explore practical strategies to help you navigate networking with confidence. Whether you're a recent graduate trying to land your first role, an experienced leader seeking partnerships, or an entrepreneur expanding your influence, this resource is designed to help you make real, lasting connections in a rapidly evolving professional landscape.

Understanding the Foundations of Modern Networking

Networking is fundamentally about creating meaningful professional connections that foster mutual growth, exchange of ideas, and access to resources. It goes beyond casual introductions. True networking involves intentional relationship-building that is maintained over time.

There are multiple modes of networking to explore:

- **In-Person Networking:** This involves attending events such as conferences, business expos, industry mixers, and professional meetups. These face-to-face interactions create deeper, more memorable connections, allowing professionals to establish trust, exchange ideas, and build genuine rapport that can lead to long-term business opportunities, partnerships, and collaborative relationships

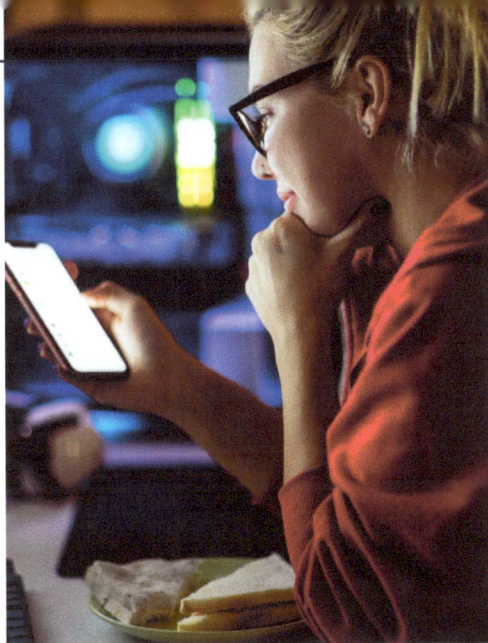

- **Online Networking:** This enables professionals to connect, engage, and collaborate through platforms like LinkedIn, Twitter/X, and industry-specific forums. It removes geographical barriers, fosters continuous dialogue, and allows for relationship-building at scale, making it easier to share insights, discover opportunities, and stay visible in your field regardless of location.

- Hybrid Events: Hybrid events combine the accessibility of virtual platforms with the personal connection of face-to-face interaction. Whether attending remotely or in person, participants can build meaningful relationships, access wider networks, and engage at their comfort level—making this format ideal for professionals seeking flexibility without sacrificing quality networking opportunities.

Effective networking keeps you plugged into your industry's latest developments and best practices. It positions you as a thought leader and builds your personal brand. For jobseekers, it opens hidden opportunities. For entrepreneurs, it attracts partners, investors, and customers.

Networking also enriches your perspective by connecting you with diverse professionals, giving you insight into how other industries tackle challenges and uncover innovation.

Unlocking the Benefits of Networking

Networking pays off in countless ways:

- **Access to Opportunities:** Access to opportunities often hinges on who you know. Many roles are filled through internal referrals or word of mouth before they're ever posted publicly. A strong, active network ensures you're in the loop—positioning you to hear about exclusive openings and get recommended for roles that align with your goals.

- **Professional Relationships:** Professional relationships built through networking extend beyond simple introductions. They foster trust, collaboration, and long-term support. Whether it's a

mentor offering guidance, a peer sharing insights, or a client opening new business doors, these connections become invaluable resources that contribute to personal growth, career development, and sustained business success.

- **Business Development:** Business development thrives on strong networks. Connections made through networking can lead to qualified leads, strategic partnerships, and investor interest. These relationships often emerge organically through trust and shared goals, turning casual conversations into concrete business opportunities that fuel growth, drive revenue, and enhance your company's long-term competitiveness.

- **Insight and Inspiration:** Insight and inspiration often come from diverse conversations. Networking exposes you to different industries, perspectives, and problem-solving approaches. These cross-sector exchanges can spark new ideas, challenge assumptions, and lead to innovative solutions - helping you think beyond your immediate context and stay agile in an ever-evolving professional landscape.

- **Personal Growth:** Personal growth is a powerful byproduct of networking. Engaging with others sharpens your communication, strengthens your emotional intelligence, and builds confidence in professional settings. Each interaction is an opportunity to practice active listening, articulate your value, and

step into leadership roles that broaden both your perspective and personal development.

The secret to effective networking lies in depth, not breadth. Nurturing a select group of meaningful, mutually beneficial relationships leads to greater trust and long-term support. Unlike superficial connections, a tight-knit network of active allies can offer real insight, valuable referrals, and consistent opportunities that drive lasting professional growth.

How to Network Effectively in a Modern World

Thriving in today's networking landscape means being intentional and authentic. It's not about collecting contacts - it's about building real connections. Here's how to approach networking with purpose and impact.

- **Define Clear Objectives:** Before engaging in any networking activity, be clear about your goals. Are you seeking mentorship, exploring collaboration, or looking for job opportunities? Knowing your purpose helps you identify the right events to attend, the people to connect with, and the conversations to initiate - making your efforts more focused, intentional, and ultimately more rewarding.

- **Select the Right Venues:** Effective networking starts with being in the right place. Choose events, forums, or platforms where your target audience is active. For instance, a tech entrepreneur might find valuable connections at startup pitch nights, accelerator meetups, or within SaaS-focused online communities. By immersing yourself in environments aligned with your goals, you increase the likelihood of engaging with relevant, like-minded professionals who can support your journey.

- **Prepare Your Elevator Pitch:** Craft a concise, authentic introduction that clearly communicates who you are, what you do, and what drives you. Keep it under 30 seconds and tailor it to your audience. Whether you're introducing yourself at a networking event or connecting online, a compelling elevator pitch makes a memorable first impression and sets the tone for deeper, more meaningful

professional conversations. Practice it until it feels natural.

- **Be Approachable and Engaging:** A warm smile, open body language, and attentive eye contact go a long way in

making others feel at ease. Listen actively, don't just wait to speak, and ask thoughtful questions that show real curiosity about the person's work, goals, or experiences. People remember how you make them feel, so fostering positive, authentic interactions is key to building strong, lasting connections.

- **Follow Up With Purpose:** After meeting someone, don't let the connection fade. Within a day or two, send a thoughtful message referencing your conversation—highlight shared interests, offer a useful link, or suggest a follow-up chat.

A personalized LinkedIn note or email reinforces your interest and professionalism, helping to cement the relationship and lay the groundwork for future collaboration, support, or opportunities. Consistent, meaningful follow-up builds lasting professional bonds.

- **Join Industry Groups:** Becoming part of a professional association or niche industry group opens the door to valuable connections and curated opportunities. These communities often host exclusive events, webinars, and discussion forums where you can meet like-minded professionals, stay updated on industry trends, and demonstrate thought leadership. Active participation not only strengthens your credibility but also helps you stay visible and engaged within your professional ecosystem.

- **Stay Authentic:** Genuine connections stem from being yourself. People are drawn to authenticity, not rehearsed pitches or salesy personas. Share your story honestly, express your challenges and goals openly, and engage with curiosity rather than agenda. Approach each interaction with the mindset of contributing value - whether through insight, support, or simply listening. Over time, authenticity builds trust, and trust is the foundation of every lasting business relationship.

Modern networking thrives on consistency and trust, not quick exchanges. Instead of viewing contacts as transactions, focus on nurturing meaningful relationships over time. Digital tools like Notion, Airtable, or even CRM platforms can help you organize your network, log key conversations, and schedule periodic check-ins. This thoughtful follow-up shows you value the relationship, keeps the connection active, and positions you as a reliable, relationship-driven professional in your industry.

Overcoming Networking Challenges With Confidence

Even experienced professionals can hit roadblocks in networking - whether it's discomfort, time constraints, or lack of clarity. The key is recognizing these challenges and applying practical strategies to move forward.

- **Conquering Shyness:** Conquering shyness begins with small, manageable steps. Attend smaller, low-pressure events or reconnect with familiar contacts to ease into networking. Prepare a few go-to conversation starters or questions beforehand. Over time, repeated exposure and positive interactions will build your confidence and make networking feel more natural and rewarding.

- **Expanding Outside Your Circle:** Expanding outside your circle means actively seeking perspectives beyond your usual environment. Attend interdisciplinary panels, community meetups, or interest-based forums to meet people from different sectors. This broadens your network, fosters innovation, and exposes you to ideas and opportunities that wouldn't typically arise within your immediate professional sphere.

- **Building Deeper Relationships:** Building deeper relationships requires intentional follow-up. After an initial meeting, share a relevant article, podcast, or idea that connects to your discussion.

This thoughtful gesture shows genuine interest. Schedule virtual coffee chats or one-on-one check-ins to continue the dialogue, strengthen the connection, and move the relationship from surface-level to meaningful and mutually beneficial.

- **Making Follow-Ups Count:** Making follow-ups count means personalizing your message. Instead of a generic note, reference something specific you discussed - like a shared interest or challenge. Propose a meaningful next step, such as exploring a partnership, exchanging insights, or scheduling a follow-up call. Thoughtful outreach reinforces the connection and opens the door for deeper engagement.

- **Staying Organized:** Staying organized is key to nurturing professional relationships. Use CRM tools, Trello boards, or even a basic spreadsheet to log contact details, meeting dates, follow-up reminders, and shared interests. This system ensures timely check-ins, prevents forgotten connections, and helps you personalize future interactions—making your networking efforts more intentional and impactful.

Networking gets easier with consistent practice. As you engage more, your confidence naturally grows especially when you begin to see real connections forming. View each interaction as an opportunity to learn, exchange value, and build genuine relationships - not just deliver a pitch.

Make Networking a Lifelong Practice

In today's hyper-connected, opportunity-rich world, networking is more than a business buzzword—it's a cornerstone of professional longevity and impact. By investing in genuine relationships, sharing your expertise, and staying open to others' stories, you set yourself up for continued growth and success.

Whether it's an introduction that leads to your dream job, a conversation that inspires a business idea, or a connection that becomes a lasting mentor, networking has the power to transform your path.

Make it a habit. Make it human. And most importantly, make it matter.

This can be accomplished by selecting a solution specifically for your industry and providing proper training to your employees, so compliance ceases being an onus but is successfully interwoven into the smooth running of your operation.

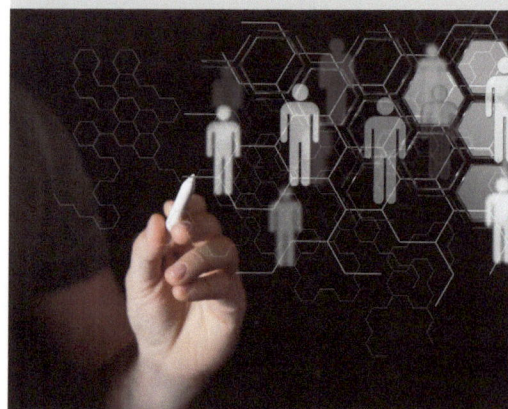

How to Be a Productive Remote Worker: A Practical Guide for the Modern Era

Remote work has evolved from a stopgap measure into a permanent and strategic approach embraced by companies and professionals worldwide. It brings undeniable perks - like flexibility, reduced commuting, and the freedom to tailor your work environment. Yet, it also presents real challenges: blurred boundaries, potential isolation, and the need for self-discipline in the absence of traditional oversight.

Whether you're a solo freelancer, a member of a global remote team, or adapting to a hybrid work model, productivity requires more than just a laptop and Wi-Fi. It demands thoughtful planning, structured habits, and a strong digital toolkit. In this updated guide, we'll cover essential routines, proven tools, and mindset strategies that empower remote professionals to stay organized, motivated, and aligned with their goals. From designing a distraction-free workspace to preserving your energy and work-life balance, this is your practical blueprint for navigating the remote landscape with focus and fulfillment no matter where you clock in.

Why Productivity Matters in Remote Work

Productivity isn't just about getting things done. It's about aligning your actions with clear goals and maintaining focus on high-impact work. In a remote environment, where home life, digital noise, and endless tabs compete for your attention, productivity demands more than willpower. It requires systems that reinforce purpose, minimize distractions, and encourage consistent progress.

For remote workers, the shift from office-based accountability to self-driven momentum can be both liberating and challenging. Without coworkers physically present or managers walking by, it becomes easy to lose track of time, overextend on minor tasks, or blur the line between work and rest. That's why building intentional habits like time blocking, using productivity tools, and taking mindful breaks is essential.

On an organizational level, teams that adopt structured remote workflows often see improved efficiency, clearer communication, and stronger performance outcomes. Individually, staying productive not only boosts performance, it also fosters a healthier work-life balance, reduces stress, and leads to greater fulfillment. When you create a setup that supports your focus, energy, and goals, you're not just checking off boxes. You're building a sustainable rhythm for doing your best work, wherever you are.

Set Realistic Expectations

Remote work isn't just about ditching the commute or working in pajamas. It's about mastering the balance between freedom and responsibility. Success comes from setting boundaries, staying focused, and maintaining daily discipline while enjoying the flexibility that remote environments offer. The key is structure that supports consistent, meaningful progress.

Tips:

- **Build a flexible yet structured schedule.** Create a schedule that provides structure without being rigid. A flexible framework gives your day direction while allowing room for adjustments. This reduces decision fatigue, helps you stay focused on priorities, and ensures you consistently make progress even when your tasks or energy levels shift throughout the day.

- **Establish daily routines.** Establishing daily routines creates a rhythm that boosts productivity and mental clarity. Morning rituals help you ease into focus, structured work sprints enhance output, and evening wind-down habits signal it's time to rest. These consistent cues train your brain to switch gears smoothly between work mode and personal time.

- **Define daily goals.** Defining daily goals keeps your workflow intentional and focused. Break larger projects into manageable chunks and identify 2–3 top priorities each morning. This approach prevents overwhelm, encourages momentum, and helps you make steady progress on

meaningful work rather than getting lost in low-value tasks or constant context-switching.

- **Limit distractions.** Minimize distractions by activating browser blockers like Freedom or Cold Turkey and silencing non-essential notifications during focused work periods. Creating a distraction-free environment helps protect your attention span, boosts concentration, and allows you to complete deep work faster and with higher quality without unnecessary digital interruptions pulling you off track.

Communicate openly. Maintain open communication by regularly sharing updates, progress, and challenges with your team. Whether through daily stand-ups, status reports, or quick messages, transparency fosters trust, ensures alignment, and helps address obstacles early. Proactive communication keeps everyone on the same page and contributes to a more collaborative remote work environment.

Maintain Work-Life Balance

Remote work often blurs the lines between personal life and professional responsibilities, making it easy to overwork or remain constantly "on." Creating clear boundaries, like a dedicated workspace, scheduled work hours, and consistent end-of-day routines, helps protect your well-being. This separation is crucial for sustaining long-term productivity and avoiding the creeping onset of burnout.

Tips:

- **Set clear boundaries.** Set clear boundaries by designating specific work hours and sticking to them. Create a physical workspace, even if it's just a corner of a room, to mentally shift into work mode. When the day ends, disconnect fully. Log off, silence notifications, and step away to recharge without guilt.

- **Prioritize breaks.** Prioritize breaks throughout your day to reset your focus and maintain energy. Step outside for a short walk, stretch your body, or take a few minutes to meditate. These small pauses reduce mental fatigue, improve circulation, and help you return to tasks with greater clarity and creativity.

- **Stay active.** Stay active by integrating regular movement into your day. Whether it's a quick home workout, a lunchtime walk, or simple stretching between tasks, physical activity

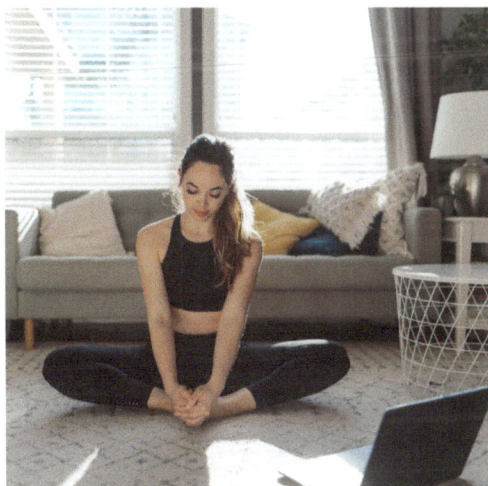

boosts circulation, sharpens focus, and enhances overall energy. Movement also breaks the monotony of screen time, helping you feel refreshed and ready to tackle work.

- **Log off on time.** Log off on time to protect your personal time and mental health. Powering down your devices at the end of the workday signals a clear boundary between work and rest. It helps you recharge, avoid burnout, and maintain a sustainable routine especially when working remotely blurs those lines.

- **Stay connected socially.** Stay connected socially by carving out time for meaningful conversations with friends and loved ones. Remote work can feel isolating, so nurturing personal relationships is vital. Whether it's a quick video call, a walk with a friend, or a family dinner, regular connection keeps your emotional well-being strong.

Get Organized

An organized digital and physical workspace minimizes distractions and boosts clarity. Keep your desktop tidy, close unused tabs, and sort files regularly. In your physical space, reduce clutter, keep essentials within reach, and personalize it for comfort. A clean environment helps your mind focus and enhances daily productivity.

Tips:

- **Declutter your desk.** Declutter your desk to create a calm, focused environment. Remove items you don't use daily and keep only what's essential like your laptop, notebook, and a water bottle. A clean, intentional workspace supports better concentration, reduces stress, and helps you start each day with a clear, organized mindset.

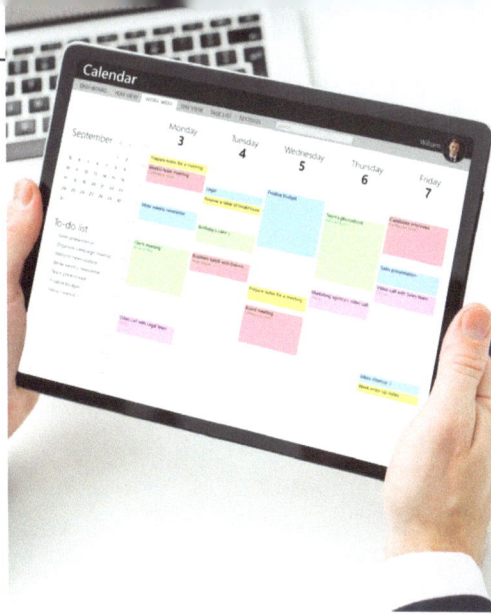

- **Use a planner or task manager.** Use a planner or task manager to offload mental clutter and stay on track. Whether you prefer digital tools like Notion or Todoist, or a simple paper notebook, capturing tasks and deadlines in one place helps you focus, prioritize effectively, and reduce the stress of remembering everything.

- **Prioritize daily.** Prioritize daily by reviewing your to-do list each morning. Identify what's urgent, what's important, and what can wait. This habit keeps you aligned with shifting goals and helps you start the day with clarity and intention ensuring your energy goes toward what matters most.

- **Store files smartly.** Store files smartly by using cloud-based platforms like Google Drive or Dropbox. Organize documents into clearly labeled, intuitive folders to avoid clutter and save time.

A well-structured digital workspace enhances productivity, simplifies collaboration, and ensures that important information is always accessible when you need it.

Delegate and Outsource

Trying to do everything leads to inefficiency. Focus on your strengths and delegate the rest.

Tips:

- **Know your zone of genius.** Those tasks that energize you and bring the highest impact. Focus your time and energy on these strengths to boost productivity and fulfillment

- **Lean on your team.** Collaboration leads to stronger outcomes and eases the pressure. Delegate, brainstorm, and support one another to stay motivated, aligned, and efficient in remote environments.

- **Hire help.** Hire help when needed. Delegating repetitive or time-consuming administrative tasks to freelancers or virtual assistants can free up your schedule for more strategic work. Platforms like Upwork or Fiverr make it easy to find skilled professionals who can handle everything from scheduling to research.

This not only boosts your productivity but also allows you to focus on high-impact tasks that drive results. Invest in support to work smarter, not harder.

Take Meaningful Breaks

Breaks are essential to sustained productivity. Taking time to step away, stretch, or reset your mind can boost creativity, reduce stress, and help you return to tasks with renewed focus.

Tips:

- **Take a real lunch break.** Step away from your desk, avoid screens, and focus on enjoying your meal. Giving your brain a true pause helps you return sharper and more focused.

- **Go outside.** A dose of sunshine and fresh air can lift your mood, spark new ideas, and refresh your focus especially during a midday slump or creative block.

- **Give your eyes a break.** Follow the 20-20-20 rule: every 20 minutes, look at something 20 feet away for 20 seconds. It helps reduce eye strain and refresh your focus.

- **Practice mindfulness.** Even a quick 5-minute meditation can improve focus, reduce stress, and help you reset. Use apps like Headspace or Calm to build the habit into your day.

Use the Right Tools

Technology can be a powerful ally or a major distraction. Choose tools that streamline your workflow, minimize interruptions, and help you stay organized, focused, and in control of your day.

Productivity Tools:

- Use tools like **Asana, Trello, or ClickUp** to organize tasks, manage deadlines, and track project progress. These platforms keep everything visible, helping you stay accountable and on top of priorities.

- **Toggl and RescueTime** help you understand how your time is spent. Use them to track hours, identify productivity gaps, and make smarter decisions about where to focus your energy.

- **Slack, Zoom, and Microsoft Teams** enable seamless communication and collaboration. Whether you're chatting, video calling, or managing projects in channels, these tools keep remote teams connected and aligned in real time.

- **Notion, Evernote, and Bear** are powerful tools for capturing ideas, organizing notes, and managing content. They streamline workflows, making it easier to store, access, and structure information efficiently.

- **Freedom and Cold Turkey** are distraction-blocking apps that help you stay focused by limiting access to time-wasting websites and apps. Use them during deep work sessions to protect your productivity.

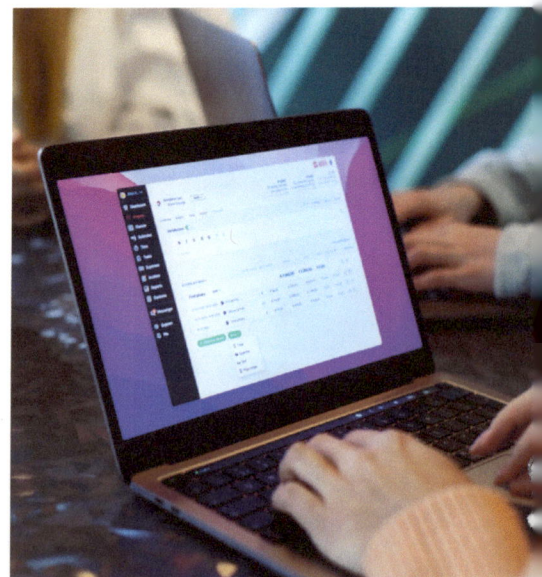

Communicate Proactively

Strong communication is the backbone of successful remote work. It keeps teams aligned, builds trust, and ensures that everyone is working toward the same goals no matter where they're located.

Tips:

- **Over-communicate when in doubt.** It's better to repeat important details than risk misunderstandings. Clear, consistent updates keep everyone on the same page and help prevent delays or missed expectations.

- **Use multiple formats.** Pair quick chats with detailed emails and regular video calls to ensure clarity. Different messages need different mediums—choose the right one to match the message and context.

- Set meeting agendas. Share a clear outline beforehand to guide the discussion and keep meetings on track.

This ensures productive conversations and shows respect for everyone's time and attention.

- **Check in regularly.** Whether through daily standups or weekly syncs, consistent check-ins foster alignment, build trust, and provide space to surface questions, updates, or challenges before they escalate.

Stay Motivated and Engaged

Motivation can waver in isolation. Establish energizing rituals, celebrate small wins, and build systems that keep momentum and purpose alive.

Tips:

- **Celebrate every win.** Acknowledge progress, track milestones, and take time to recognize what you've achieved—it fuels motivation and builds momentum.

- **Revisit your purpose regularly.** Reflecting on why your work matters renews motivation, sharpens focus, and brings meaning to daily tasks.

- **Stay inspired.** Listen to podcasts, read books, or learn a new skill.

- **Socialize with peers.** Light conversations boost morale, spark creativity, and remind you that you're not alone.

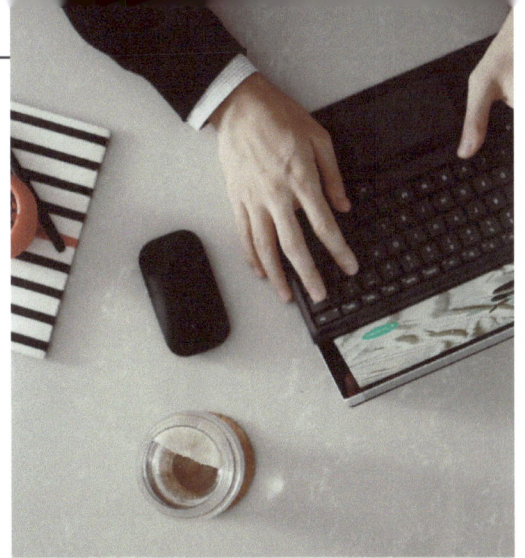

Being a productive remote worker isn't about cramming more into your day. It's about focusing on what moves the needle and doing it with clarity and consistency. It means building routines that support your energy, setting boundaries that protect your time, and using tools that reduce friction instead of adding to it.

Productivity flourishes when you align your work with your strengths, structure your day intentionally, and stay connected with your team and goals. Remote work opens the door to flexibility, but success within that freedom requires discipline and awareness. Your workspace, your schedule, and even your mindset all shape how effectively you operate.

There's no one-size-fits-all approach, but the key is to experiment, adjust, and commit to what works for you. With the right habits and environment in place, remote work becomes more than just a change of scenery. It becomes a catalyst for both professional growth and personal balance.

How To Execute a Successful Launch in Today's Market

Launching a new product, service, or brand is one of the most energizing moments in any business journey. It's a culmination of research, development, and vision all channeled into a single point of entry to the market. But behind every smooth launch is a long runway of preparation. It's not just about a splashy debut or eye-catching announcement, it's about validating a real need, positioning the offer clearly, and orchestrating every moving part from messaging to logistics.

A successful launch can generate momentum, attract early adopters, and set the tone for long-term growth. On the flip side, a rushed or misaligned launch can lead to missed opportunities, poor customer experience, or even reputational damage. That's why the best launches aren't improvised. they're designed. They involve cross-functional alignment, well-defined goals, contingency planning, and a post-launch follow-up strategy to maintain traction once the buzz settles.

Whether you're bringing your first product to life or expanding an established brand portfolio, the fundamentals remain the same: know your audience, lead with value, and build anticipation intentionally. The launch is your first impression. It needs to deliver clarity, credibility, and connection from the very first touchpoint. While the journey may look different for every entrepreneur or team, the principles of an effective launch are universal and mastering them can be the difference between a quiet rollout and a breakthrough moment.

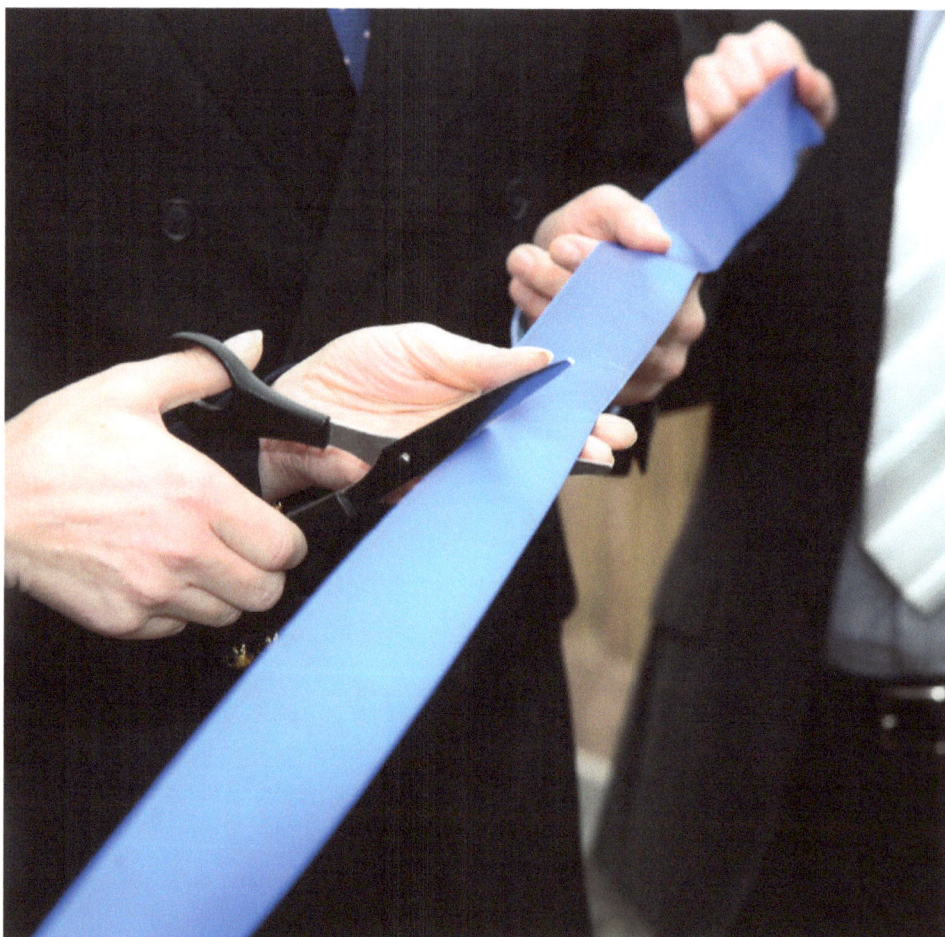

4 Core Steps to a Successful Launch

Identify a Real Problem

The foundation of a great launch is rooted in solving a real, tangible problem. Before developing your product or campaign, take time to

understand your audience's pain points. Conduct interviews, run surveys, and study industry trends. If your offer doesn't address a specific need, it will struggle to gain traction no matter how flashy your marketing is.

Design a Market-Ready Solution

With a validated problem in hand, design a solution that not only addresses it, but does so in a unique, value-driven way. Research your competitors thoroughly. What do they do well? Where do they fall short? Use this insight to position your product strategically and craft a compelling unique value proposition (UVP).

Build a Launch Plan

Now it's time to build your go-to-market (GTM) strategy. This includes setting launch objectives, outlining tactics (e.g. email marketing, paid ads, influencer outreach), assembling your launch team, and

establishing a timeline. Create a detailed calendar with milestones, deliverables, and deadlines.

Execute the Launch

Your launch day should feel like the crescendo of a well-rehearsed performance not a last-minute scramble. Ensure all tech is tested, assets are live, and your team is ready to monitor performance in real time. Be prepared to adapt quickly based on feedback and analytics.

Why Launches Matter

A great launch is more than a kickoff. It's a defining moment that shapes perception, builds trust, and sets the foundation for everything that comes next. It signals to your audience that you're serious, strategic, and ready to deliver. A well-executed launch doesn't just introduce a product or service. t creates a narrative, generates buzz, and draws in early believers who become brand advocates. It creates excitement, clarity, and momentum that extends beyond the initial announcement. When done right, a strong launch

builds credibility, captures attention, and sets your business on a path toward long-term growth, loyalty, and lasting market presence.

What Makes a Launch Successful?

While every launch is unique, successful ones share a few key ingredients:

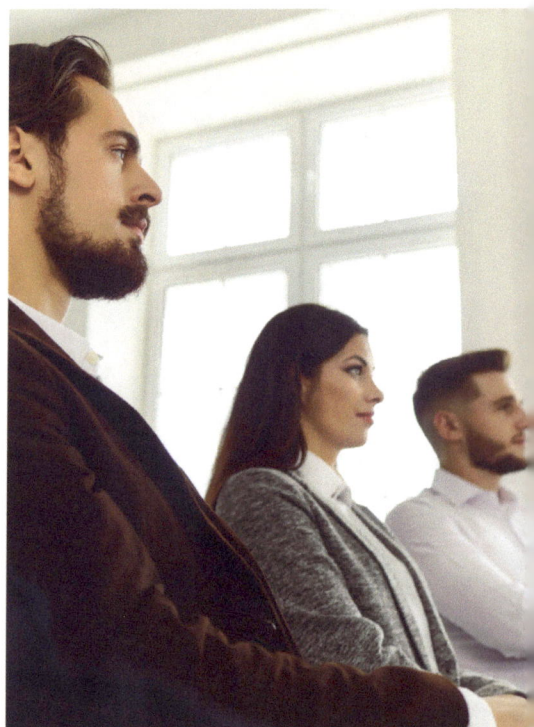

Know Your Audience

Identifying your ideal customer is the cornerstone of any successful launch. Understand their values, pain points, and online behavior. Customize your messaging, visuals, and outreach to resonate deeply with them. When your launch speaks directly to their needs and preferences, engagement increases and so does the likelihood of lasting brand loyalty.

Set Realistic Goals

Success isn't one-size-fits-all. Whether your aim is to acquire your first 100 users, land media coverage, or secure early sales, define clear, measurable goals from the start. These benchmarks serve as your launch compass, helping you prioritize efforts, track performance, and keep everyone on the same page. When your team is aligned on what success looks like, you're far more likely to achieve it and know when you've arrived.

Understand the Competitive Landscape

Thorough research lays the foundation for a successful launch. Understand your competitive landscape - who your rivals are, what they're offering, how they're positioning themselves, and where they've fallen short. This intel empowers you to craft a unique value proposition, sidestep common pitfalls, and identify untapped opportunities. Smart research not only informs your messaging and pricing. It also gives you the confidence to launch with clarity and a strategic edge.

Pick the Right Time

Timing can make or break a launch. Align your efforts with market trends, seasonal demand, and your team's bandwidth. A rushed launch often leads to missed opportunities and preventable errors. Instead, choose a moment when your audience is most receptive and your business is fully prepared to deliver on its promise.

Choose the Right Platform or Location

Choose a launch platform that maximizes impact. Whether it's a trade show, website rollout, or livestream event, align your venue with where your audience already engages. The right setting enhances visibility, encourages participation, and ensures your message reaches the people most likely to care and act.

Generate Press and Media Buzz

Start building buzz well before launch day. Reach out to journalists, secure early media coverage, and coordinate with influencers aligned with your brand. Developing these relationships weeks in advance ensures you have advocates ready to amplify your message when it matters most, helping your launch gain momentum from the very beginning.

Maximize Social Media Impact

Harness social media to create a narrative around your launch. Share sneak peeks, run countdowns, post behind-the-scenes moments, and host live Q&As to spark curiosity and encourage interaction.

This steady stream of engaging content builds momentum, strengthens audience connection, and ensures your launch doesn't just appear, it arrives with impact.

Pre-Launch Essentials: What You Shouldn't Skip

Ensure Your Website Is Ready

Your website must be polished and reliable. Optimize for speed, mobile responsiveness, and SEO performance. Double-check that every link, form, and checkout

process functions flawlessly to avoid user frustration. A smooth, professional experience builds trust and converts curiosity into action especially during the critical moments of your launch.

Build a Strategic Marketing Plan

A well-structured launch plan should clearly define your positioning, key messaging, and the channels you'll use to reach your audience. Map out a detailed promotional timeline, set measurable KPIs, and establish tools or systems to track performance across platforms. This ensures accountability and helps you optimize in real time.

Don't Miss Deadlines

Treat your launch like a strategic campaign. Use project management tools like Notion, Trello, or Asana to break down tasks, assign responsibilities, and maintain clear timelines.

Regular check-ins and transparent workflows ensure accountability, prevent last-minute chaos, and keep every moving part aligned toward a successful, on-time launch.

Sync Your Social Media Accounts

Ensure every marketing channel reflects consistent branding and messaging around your launch. From social media to email, align visuals and voice. Pre-schedule content for smoother execution, incorporate relevant hashtags for reach, and stay responsive - engaging with comments and conversations builds momentum and signals that your team is present and listening.

Avoiding Launch Day Chaos: How to Minimize Risk

Test Everything

Conduct mock launches to simulate the full user journey from landing page to checkout. Test your email automations, links, payment systems, and messaging for clarity and

functionality. Identify and fix glitches or bottlenecks early to ensure a smooth, frustration-free experience for your audience when the real launch goes live.

Focus on the Fundamentals

Stay grounded in your customer's pain points, the value your product delivers, and how you uniquely fit in the market. If any element feels off - messaging, pricing, or channel - adjust quickly.

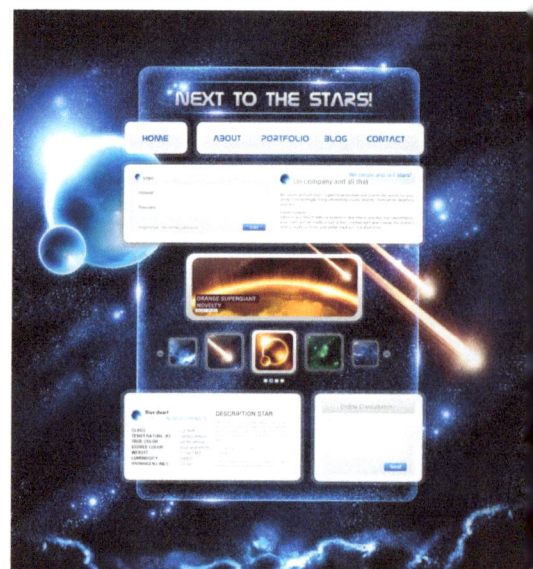

Alignment ensures your launch resonates, builds trust, and drives meaningful traction from day one. Always lead with relevance and clarity.

Start Small, Then Scale

Start with a soft launch to test the waters and gather feedback from a smaller, engaged audience. This controlled rollout allows you to identify and fix issues, fine-tune your messaging, and validate your offer ensuring a stronger, more confident full-scale launch that resonates with your broader market.

Prepare for Support Needs

Establish clear systems for handling customer questions, technical hiccups, and fulfillment processes. Have support channels ready whether chat, email, or phone and make response times a priority. A quick, professional resolution to issues builds trust and protects your reputation during a high-visibility moment like a launch. Preparedness shows you take your customers seriously

Build Anticipation with Pre-Marketing

Build anticipation by strategically releasing content before launch. Use email waitlists to capture interest early, share sneak peeks to spark curiosity, and run countdowns across your channels. This drip approach nurtures engagement, warms up your audience, and ensures you're not launching to silence but to an eager, informed community.

Set Realistic Expectations

Setting realistic expectations builds long-term trust. Be transparent about your product's current capabilities, upcoming features, and any known limitations. Let customers know where to find support and what to expect post-launch. Overdelivering on honest

promises creates stronger loyalty than overhyping and underdelivering, a reputation safeguard as your business continues to grow.

Examples of Remarkable Product Launches

Here are a few standout launches that raised the bar:

- **Amazon Echo** redefined smart living by introducing a voice-activated assistant that felt intuitive and futuristic. Its sleek design, seamless integration with everyday tasks, and expanding ecosystem of Alexa skills made it an instant hit. The Echo didn't just launch a product—it launched a new way to interact with technology at home.

- **Apple Watch Series 3** elevated the smartwatch category by merging fitness tracking, heart rate monitoring, and cellular connectivity with sleek, minimalist design. It wasn't just a timepiece—it became a personal wellness companion, allowing users to stay active, connected, and informed without needing their phone in hand at all times.

- **Tesla's Cybertruck** reveal captured global attention with its unconventional design and unforgettable window mishap. The spectacle sparked viral buzz, showcasing the power of bold branding and theatrical product reveals. Despite polarizing opinions, the launch generated massive media coverage and tens of thousands of pre-orders—proving controversy can fuel commercial momentum.

- **Clubhouse's invite-only rollout strategy** created a sense of scarcity and exclusivity, fueling curiosity and word-of-mouth buzz. By limiting access early on,

the app cultivated demand, sparked FOMO, and positioned itself as a must-have platform—especially among influencers, tech insiders, and creatives eager to be part of the next big thing.

- **Airbnb's rebrand and strategic expansion** marked a shift from simple lodging to a lifestyle brand rooted in belonging. Launching just as travelers sought authentic, flexible experiences, the refreshed identity and platform features helped Airbnb tap into new markets, redefine travel expectations, and solidify its position as a global hospitality leader.

Sustaining Post-Launch Momentum

A successful launch doesn't end at the announcement. Your next phase should include:

- Gathering user feedback

- Releasing product updates or new content

- Following up with press and influencers

- Launching retargeting campaigns

- Measuring what worked and optimizing what didn't

The most successful businesses understand that a launch isn't a one-day affair. It's the start of a broader, ongoing growth cycle. It's not just about going live; it's about staying alive in the minds of your customers. Treating a launch as a dynamic, multi-phase journey allows you to gather momentum, collect feedback, refine messaging, and evolve alongside your market.

A well-executed launch sets the tone, but the follow-through is what drives long-term success. Businesses that win don't just show up once. they continue to show up consistently, iterating based on real user insights and expanding their reach strategically. They integrate launches into broader marketing, sales, and customer success initiatives. Each campaign builds upon the last, compounding awareness, trust, and loyalty.

When executed with intention, a launch acts as a catalyst sparking conversation, inspiring engagement, and creating community. When carried forward with agility, it opens doors to new partnerships, innovations, and revenue streams. This is how great businesses grow, not by celebrating a moment, but by building a movement. The launch becomes the ignition point, and what follows is the real journey: nurturing a brand that adapts, resonates, and thrives over time.

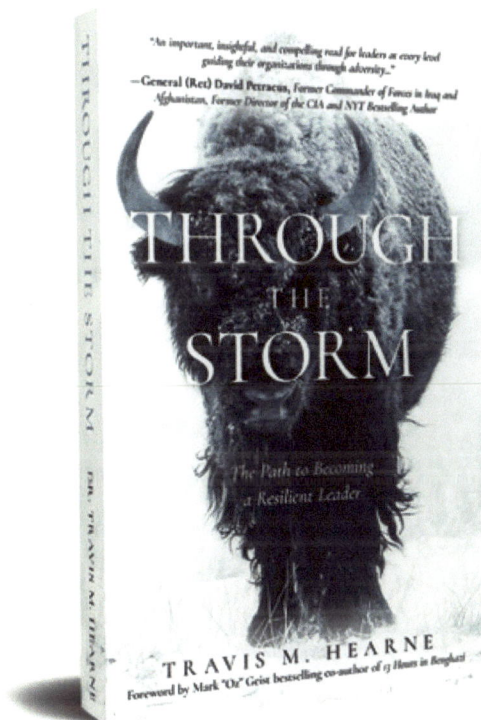

Revolutionize Marketing: Profit-Boosting Tactics

In today's fast-paced digital world, standing out in the marketplace requires far more than traditional marketing tactics. For modern entrepreneurs and business leaders, effective marketing must be strategic, responsive, and rooted in the latest technology. The era of generic ads and broad messaging is over. Today's consumers are savvy, selective, and expect more - more personalization, more authenticity, and more alignment with their values.

They want to feel seen, heard, and understood. That means your brand can't afford to rely on outdated approaches. Success hinges on your ability to deliver tailored experiences that speak directly to your audience's needs and aspirations. Whether it's through AI-powered targeting, content that adds real value, or sustainable messaging that aligns with conscious consumerism, your marketing must be both thoughtful and dynamic.

This article explores the most effective marketing strategies of the moment, from leveraging advanced data analytics and automation to incorporating ethical storytelling and hybrid channel strategies.

These tactics aren't just designed to increase short-term clicks or conversions. They're built to foster deeper relationships, long-term loyalty, and sustainable profit growth. If you're looking to future-proof your brand and lead with purpose, these marketing principles are your competitive edge.

Understanding Your Audience Deeply

Marketing success begins with a deep, nuanced understanding of your audience far beyond age, location, or job title. Truly effective marketing digs into the why behind consumer behavior: what drives their decisions, what challenges they face, what content creation to product development. The more specific and informed these personas are, the more relevant your campaigns will be. And in a saturated digital marketplace, relevance is what cuts through the noise. It drives higher engagement, improves conversion rates, and ultimately leads to better returns on your marketing investment. Understanding your audience isn't just helpful. It's foundational.

Digital Transformation in Marketing

Digital tools have completely transformed the marketing landscape, empowering brands to connect with customers faster, smarter, and more personally than ever before. Automation platforms allow businesses to manage campaigns efficiently - delivering the right message to the right audience at the right time. AI-driven solutions enhance this further, offering predictive insights, real-time

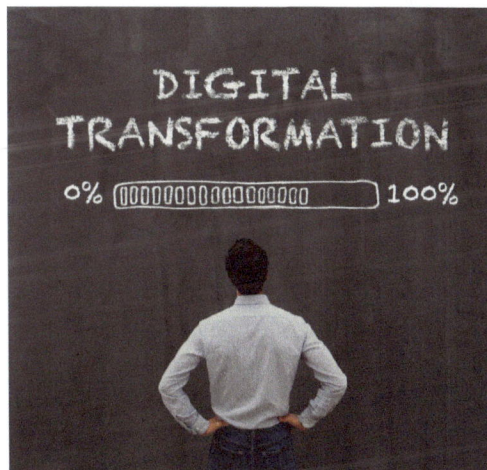

personalization, and data-backed decision-making. With these tools, brands can craft seamless email sequences, segment audiences with precision, and nurture leads through intuitive CRM pipelines.

Social media platforms have become more than just broadcast channels. They're

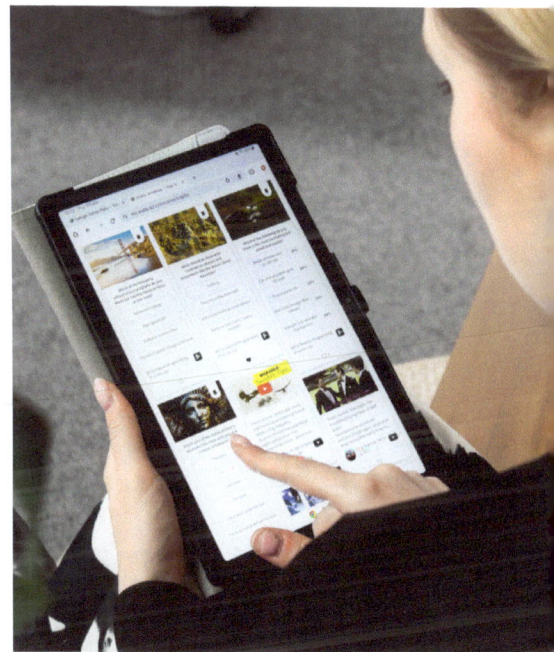

vibrant hubs of conversation and community. Whether you're using TikTok for short-form storytelling, Instagram for visual engagement, or LinkedIn for thought leadership, each offers a direct connection to your audience. The key is knowing how to use these platforms not just to push content, but to listen, respond, and build meaningful relationships.

Meanwhile, analytics tools such as Google Analytics, HubSpot, or native social insights help marketers continuously improve.

values they care about, and where they spend their time online. It's about discovering unmet needs and tapping into emotional motivators that generic campaigns often miss.

To do this, businesses must leverage both quantitative and qualitative data. Surveys can uncover preferences and expectations, while analytics tools reveal patterns in behavior, like how users navigate your website or what content they engage with most. CRM platforms help track individual interactions and buying history, offering valuable context for personalized outreach. Social listening tools give real-time insights into customer sentiment and trending conversations in your industry.

With these insights, you can build detailed, dynamic customer personas - composite profiles that guide everything from

Measuring what's working, what's not, and where adjustments can drive better outcomes. By staying agile with your tech stack and continuously testing new tools, you position your brand to respond quickly to market changes, consumer trends, and emerging opportunities. In the digital era, adaptability and personalization are the foundation of impactful marketing.

Content is King: Creating Compelling Content

Content marketing continues to be one of the most powerful tools for brand growth but the difference today lies in quality, intention, and execution. It's no longer enough to simply publish content. To truly resonate, your material must be valuable, relevant, and designed with your audience's needs in mind. Great content educates, entertains, or solves a real problem, sometimes all three at once. Whether you're creating YouTube tutorials that walk users through key processes, launching a podcast that dives into industry insights, or publishing thoughtful blog posts, your goal should be to meet your audience where they are and move them closer to a solution.

Storytelling adds emotional resonance to content, but it's strategy that gives it purpose. Start with empathy - understand what your audience is going through. Then, strengthen your narrative with research, stats, or testimonials to establish credibility. Finally, end with a clear call to action that guides your audience to the next step - whether that's signing up, sharing, or buying.

Consistency is also key. Establish a rhythm that builds trust and keeps your brand top of mind. In a crowded digital space, content that genuinely helps while aligning with business objectives becomes a powerful engine for growth, engagement, and long-term loyalty.

The Power of Influencer Marketing

Influencers bring both authenticity and reach to modern marketing strategies. In an era where consumers crave real, relatable voices over polished brand messages, influencers provide a powerful connection point. People trust the creators they follow, whether it's for product recommendations, lifestyle tips, or honest reviews, making influencer collaborations a high-ROI channel when done right. The key lies in choosing partners who genuinely align with your brand values and who already speak to the audience you want to reach.

Micro and nano-influencers, despite having smaller followings, often drive higher engagement rates, especially in niche markets.

Their audiences tend to be more tightly knit and responsive, leading to better performance per dollar spent. These smaller creators are seen as more accessible and relatable, which makes their endorsements feel like trusted word-of-mouth rather than paid promotion.

However, success doesn't come from follower count alone. Track performance metrics that matter - click-through rates, conversion rates, engagement quality, and actual sales generated. Likes and views are vanity metrics unless they lead to meaningful action. Influencer marketing, when treated as a strategic partnership rather than a transactional deal, can amplify your message, build lasting brand affinity, and convert passive viewers into loyal customers.

Sustainable and Ethical Marketing

Sustainable and ethical marketing is no longer a fringe initiative. It's a core expectation. Today's consumers are more informed, more vocal, and more invested in aligning with brands that reflect their personal values This shift means businesses must go beyond catchy taglines and embrace transparency, responsibility, and authenticity across all aspects of their marketing.

Ethical marketing is about much more than positive messaging. It includes how a brand sources its products, treats its employees, handles customer data, and engages with diverse communities. Sustainability also plays a central role. From reducing packaging waste to offsetting carbon emissions and supporting circular economy models, companies that prioritize sustainability show that they care about more than profits.

Diversity, equity, and inclusion (DEI) are equally important. Representation matters - not just in marketing campaigns, but also behind the scenes. Ethical marketing champions a broad range of voices and perspectives, and consumers are quick to spot brands that lack substance or authenticity.

In addition, data responsibility has emerged as a defining issue. With privacy concerns at an all-time high, businesses must be transparent about how they collect, store, and use customer information. Gaining trust in this area is vital.

Ethical and sustainable marketing isn't a trend. It's a competitive advantage. Brands that lead with integrity and back it up with action build deeper emotional connections with their audience. These connections translate into loyalty, advocacy, and long-term growth. In a crowded marketplace, walking your talk is the most powerful differentiator you have.

Integrating Offline and Online Marketing

While digital marketing often dominates today's conversations, it's important not to overlook the power of traditional offline channels. Events, print advertising, and direct mail still have a strong presence especially when used strategically alongside digital efforts. The most effective marketing strategies recognize that offline and online channels are not in competition. Instead, they work best when they're integrated into a cohesive, cross-channel experience that delivers consistent messaging and value.

Offline marketing shines in creating tangible, memorable touchpoints. A well-designed direct mail piece, a print ad in a local publication, or an engaging in-person event can leave a lasting impression especially when they tap into a personalized, hyper-local approach.

For example, a boutique fitness studio might mail postcards to residents within a few miles of their location, offering a free class. That same offer should appear in geo-targeted Instagram ads, and when scanned via QR code on the postcard, the customer should land on a matching landing page with clear messaging and branding.

This kind of seamless integration builds trust. Consumers today engage with brands across multiple platforms sometimes switching between offline and online several times before making a decision. Inconsistent messaging between those channels can cause confusion or even distrust. That's why it's essential to unify your brand voice, visuals, and offers across every touchpoint.

Events are another powerful offline tactic that pairs well with digital. Hosting a product launch, workshop, or networking event gives customers a direct brand experience. These in-person moments become even more powerful when amplified online before, during, and after the event. Tease the event on social media, use email campaigns to invite your audience, and create a branded hashtag to generate live buzz. After the event, share recap videos, customer testimonials, or a digital offer for attendees to take the next step. Apple is a great example of this approach, blending sleek product launch events with global livestreams, influencer content, and a website experience that reflects the same excitement and messaging.

Direct mail is also making a comeback, especially when combined with data-driven targeting. Platforms like USPS Informed Delivery or hybrid mail services allow businesses to send personalized mailers and pair them with follow-up emails or social media ads, ensuring multiple brand impressions across different channels. Including a QR code, unique promo code, or even augmented reality features can bridge the physical to the digital effortlessly.

The key is consistency. A prospect who receives a catalog or brochure should encounter the same product visuals, tone, and offers when they visit your website or social media pages. If your Instagram ad promises 20% off, your print flyer shouldn't say 15%. These small inconsistencies can break consumer trust and reduce conversions.

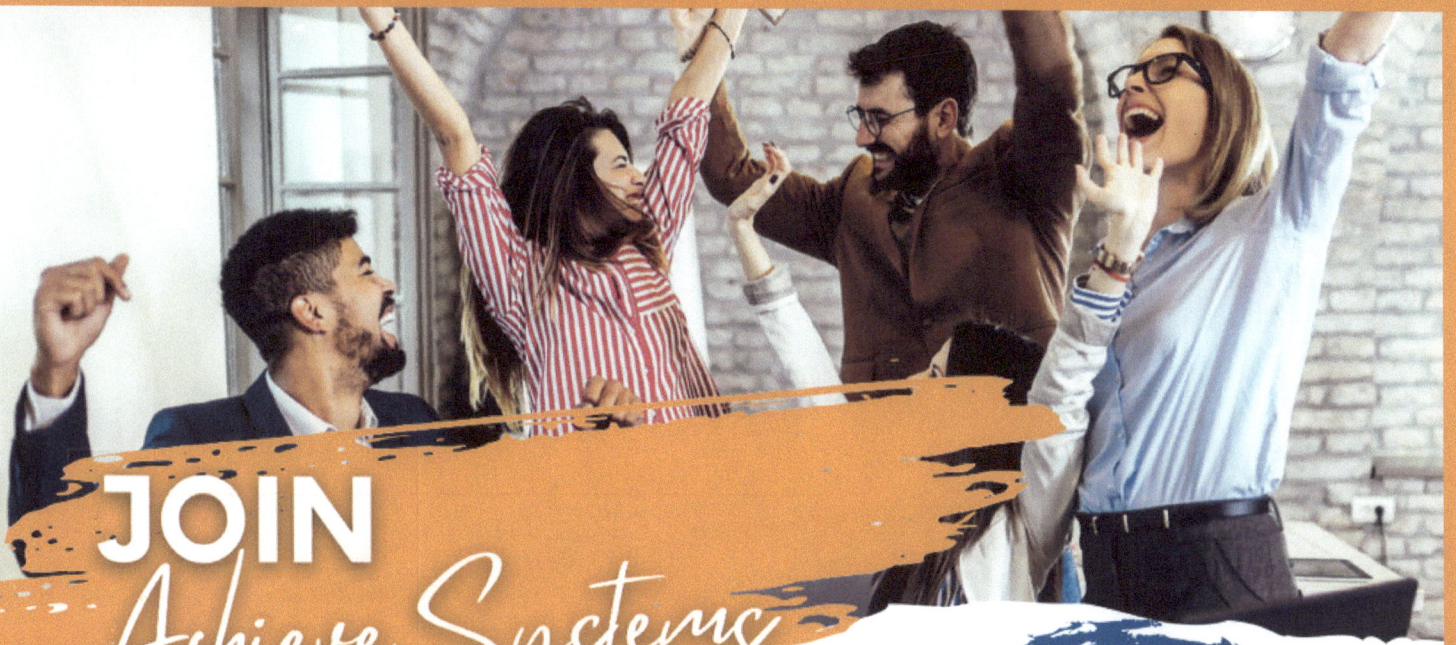

JOIN
Achieve Systems

BECOME AN ACHIEVE SYSTEMS MEMBER TODAY!

Education

We help you get the tools to create a thriving business! It's turnkey, you can start NOW!

Marketing

We provide marketing guidelines but also plug you into our conferences, events and database

Community

We have a thriving community of entrepreneurs and business owners for you to collaborate, refer and partner with to grow and up-level your business!

WE WORK WITH ENTREPRENEURS, BUSINESS OWNERS, SPEAKERS & LEADERS!

CONTACT US OR REGISTER HERE: www.AchieveSystemsPro.com

The future of marketing belongs to brands that are agile, intentional, and deeply connected to their audience. As technology evolves and customer expectations rise, success hinges on the ability to listen, adapt, and lead with clarity and purpose. Whether you're leveraging AI to personalize campaigns or crafting value-driven content that resonates, the opportunity to build lasting relationships has never been greater. But tools alone aren't enough. What matters is how you use them to create relevance, trust, and impact.

The most successful brands are those that align their marketing with their mission, stay responsive to change, and never stop learning. Consistency, creativity, and authenticity across every channel are what transform casual buyers into loyal advocates. So take these insights, experiment boldly, and evolve your strategy over time. When you lead with purpose and stay close to your audience, your marketing doesn't just survive the future. It shapes it.

The Role of a Personal Injury Attorney in Business Risk Management

Are you confident your business is fully protected against workplace accidents and potential liability issues? Managing these risks can be complex and stressful especially when it involves employee safety and legal compliance. One key resource that's often overlooked is the guidance of a personal injury attorney.

Far from being just reactive support after an incident, a personal injury attorney can play a proactive role in shaping your risk management strategy. They help identify legal vulnerabilities, advise on safety protocols, and ensure your business is prepared if an accident does occur. By partnering with an experienced attorney, you're not just responding to risk. You're actively reducing it. This kind of legal insight can safeguard your business from costly lawsuits and reputational damage, while also reinforcing a culture of safety and accountability.

We'll dive into the valuable role personal injury attorneys play in helping businesses navigate risk with confidence and care.

How Can You Prevent Workplace Accidents?

Conducting regular safety audits is essential for identifying potential workplace hazards. To conduct these audits effectively, start by creating a checklist tailored to your specific industry standards. Include checks for equipment maintenance, proper signage, and employees' adherence to safety protocols.

Complying with Occupational Safety and Health Administration (OSHA) guidelines is crucial. Regularly updating your knowledge of OSHA standards can help prevent violations that lead to hefty fines and an increased risk of workplace injuries.

Developing and maintaining an effective safety training program is vital for minimizing accidents. Design training sessions that cover all potential hazards, correct use of equipment, and emergency procedures.

Use a mix of hands-on training and digital resources to accommodate all learning styles. Regularly conduct safety drills to keep employees prepared for emergencies. Frequent drills reinforce procedures and ensure everyone knows their role during an incident.

For entrepreneurs, effective risk management involves integrating these practices into the core of their business operations. By prioritizing safety and compliance, business leaders can significantly reduce the likelihood of workplace accidents, protecting both their employees and their bottom line.

Legal Support and Defense Protect Your Business

Building a robust defense against personal injury lawsuits is crucial to protecting your business. Work closely with your attorney to gather evidence, interview witnesses, and build a strong

case. It should show your compliance with safety rules. A personal injury attorney can handle complex legal claims. They can negotiate with plaintiffs and represent your business in court if needed.

Columbia, the bustling capital of South Carolina, thrives in a dynamic business environment. Here, companies face unique challenges related to workplace safety and liability, with personal injury claims being a prevalent issue that can greatly affect operations. Personal injury claims are prevalent and can significantly impact business operations. Personal injury attorneys play a vital role in managing these risks, negotiating fair settlements, and providing strategic legal advice. Their guidance can help prevent costly lawsuits and ensure compliance with safety standards. With the support of a personal injury attorney in Columbia SC, businesses can effectively manage risks and maintain a safer work environment.

What Are Your Responsibilities Regarding Liability for Workplace Injuries?

Employer Responsibility

Understanding when and how employers can be held liable for workplace injuries is essential to minimizing legal and financial risk. Liability often arises when businesses neglect to maintain safe working conditions, fail to provide proper training, or ignore industry safety standards and regulations. By identifying these risk factors early and addressing them proactively, employers can better protect their team, avoid costly claims, and strengthen their overall workplace safety strategy.

Workers' Compensation

Efficiently managing workers' compensation claims is vital for protecting both your employees and your bottom line. Establish a clear, streamlined process for reporting and filing claims to reduce delays and confusion.

Educate your team about their rights and obligations under the law to encourage compliance and transparency. Investigate each claim thoroughly by interviewing witnesses, checking surveillance footage, and reviewing medical documentation to detect potential fraud and ensure fair, accurate resolutions.

Tips for Reducing Liability Risk with Proper Documentation:

Keep detailed records of safety inspections, employee training sessions, and accident reports. Proper documentation serves as your best defense to prove your company took all necessary precautions.

How to Choose the Right Insurance Policies?

Selecting the right insurance policies is a cornerstone of effective risk management, especially when it comes to handling personal injury claims.

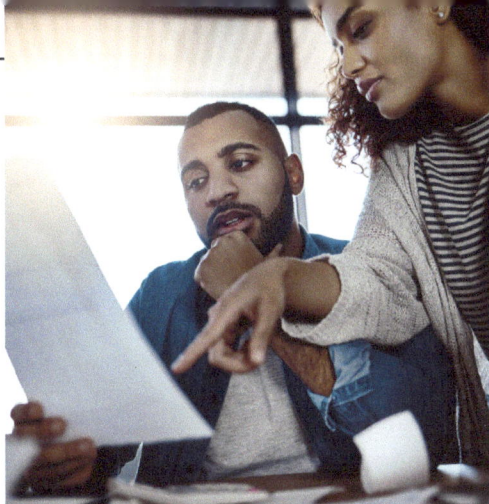

Your business should have comprehensive coverage tailored to your operations, including general liability insurance, workers' compensation, and commercial auto insurance if your employees drive for work. These policies can protect you from significant financial losses due to accidents, injuries, or lawsuits. It's important to regularly review your coverage with a trusted insurance advisor to ensure it aligns with your evolving business needs.

Equally crucial is implementing an efficient claims management system. A streamlined process, from incident reporting to final resolution, helps reduce operational downtime, contain costs, and improve outcomes. Ensure timely communication between your team, your insurance provider, and the injured party to keep the process transparent and moving forward. Strong, proactive relationships with your insurance carriers can make a significant difference in how quickly and fairly claims are resolved, minimizing disruption and stress.

Staying Updated with Laws

Staying informed about legal changes affecting business liability helps you stay compliant and reduce risks. Regularly review legal updates and consult with your attorney to understand how new laws impact your business.

Implement changes as soon as new regulations take effect and ensure all employees are trained accordingly. Adopting best practices can help maintain a safe workplace and minimize risks.

Consult professionals regularly and update your safety protocols accordingly. Ensure that your risk management policies are regularly updated to reflect the latest safety standards and best practices.

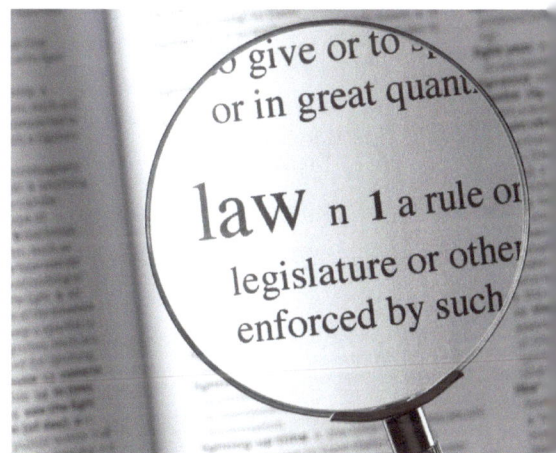

Crisis Management

Creating a well-defined response plan for personal injury incidents is essential to protecting your business, employees, and reputation. A prompt and structured approach minimizes

confusion and ensures the situation is handled with care and professionalism. Begin by outlining clear steps: administer immediate aid to the injured party, contact emergency medical services if needed, and report the incident to the appropriate internal and external parties, including your insurance provider. Conduct a thorough internal investigation to understand what happened, identify potential liabilities, and prevent future occurrences.

Your personal injury attorney plays a crucial role during this process. They provide legal guidance, ensure regulatory compliance, and manage sensitive communications with affected parties to prevent missteps that could escalate liability.

Crisis communication is just as critical. Assign a trained spokesperson to speak on behalf of the business and ensure all messages, whether internal or public, are clear, accurate, and timely. Transparency builds

trust, while misinformation or silence can damage your brand. Collaborate with PR professionals to shape the narrative and manage media inquiries thoughtfully. Keeping employees informed and supported throughout the process also reinforces a culture of accountability and care. A strong response plan not only mitigates immediate damage but also helps preserve long-term trust and credibility.

Taking Action: Building a Proactive and Legally Sound Workplace Safety Plan

Creating a safe work environment is not a one-time initiative. It's an ongoing commitment that evolves with your business. Taking action starts with recognizing that risk exists in every workplace, regardless of size or industry. The key is to be proactive, not reactive.

Start with a Thorough Risk Assessment

The first step in any effective safety plan is conducting a detailed risk assessment. This involves identifying potential hazards specific to your workplace, whether it's heavy machinery on a manufacturing floor, repetitive stress in an office setting, or exposure to hazardous materials in a lab. Once risks are identified, evaluate their likelihood and potential severity. This gives you

a roadmap for where to focus your safety efforts.

Develop and Communicate Clear Safety Policies

Based on your assessment, create comprehensive safety policies tailored to your operations. These should include procedures for equipment use, emergency protocols, injury reporting, and protective gear requirements. For example, a construction company might implement strict guidelines around fall protection and heavy machinery operation, while a retail business might focus on lifting techniques and slip-and-fall prevention.

Once these policies are created, it's critical that they're shared with your team in an understandable and accessible way.

Training and Equipment Matter

Safety measures are only effective when employees are properly trained and equipped to

MICROCASTING

Supercharge Your Business!

Do you want to find new ways to add additional income to your coaching, consulting, or content creation business?

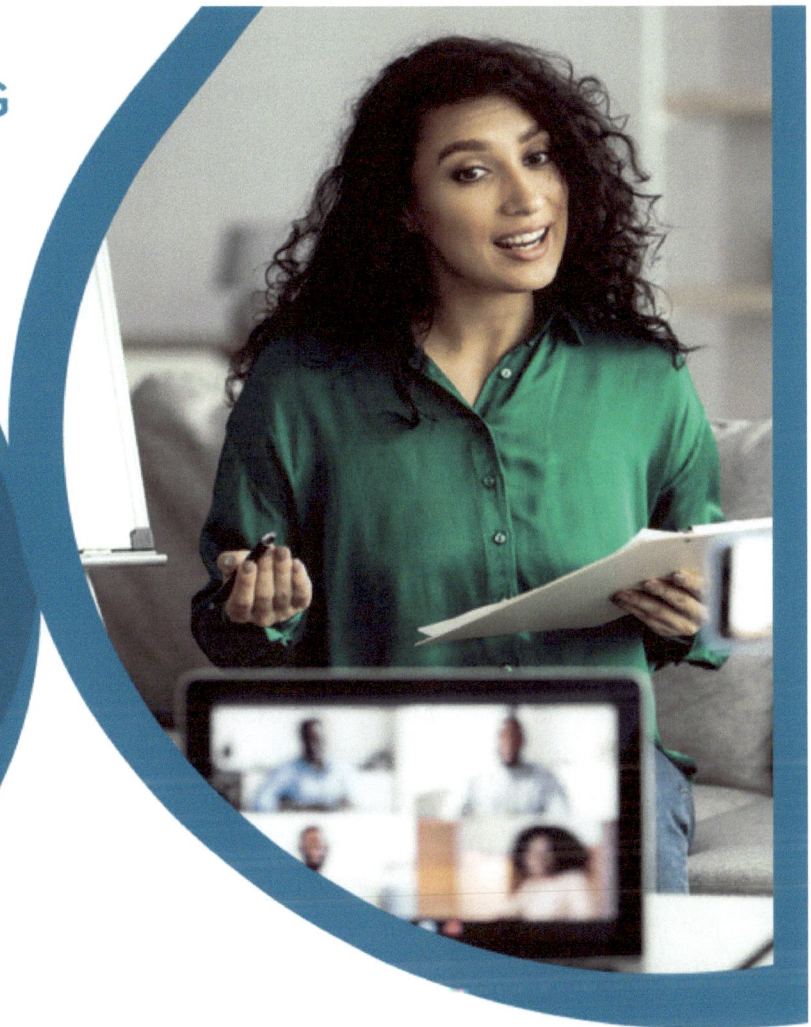

eLearning Portals by Microcasting is specifically designed for Coaches, Consultants, and Course Creators to engage your customers, establish yourself as a thought leader, and grow your revenues.

Here are just a few things you can do with **Microcasting**:

- ⊘ **Start selling** your courses and programs.
- ⊘ Create a **paid membership site** to grow your revenues.
- ⊘ Build a free membership site to **increase lead gen**.
- ⊘ Easily **integrate eLearning** into your marketing website.
- ⊘ Create **individualized customer portals** .
- ⊘ And so much more...

Microcasting is an all-in-one online learning platform that makes it easy for course creators to design, manage, and market their courses. With its personalized eLearning experience, you can keep your current customers engaged with your business, generating more upsells and higher renewal rates. Create courses quickly and effortlessly - all with the help of Microcasting!

Try Microcasting today and start transforming your business!

Request a demo - email us at ✉ info@microcasting.com **OR VISIT** 🌐 www.elearning-portals.com

follow them. Invest in onboarding sessions, regular refresher courses, and hands-on demonstrations. Provide all necessary safety gear and ensure it is well-maintained. For instance, in a food service environment, this might include training on knife safety, food handling, and proper cleaning methods to prevent contamination or injuries.

Keep It Current

Workplaces change over time - new tools, technologies, and employees bring new challenges. That's why regular reviews of your safety policies and procedures are essential. Schedule audits and walkthroughs to spot outdated protocols or emerging risks. Use incident reports and employee feedback to guide your updates and improvements.

Promote a Safety-First Culture

A culture that values safety starts from the top. Leadership must model safe behaviors and reinforce expectations. Encourage employees to speak up about safety concerns and treat every report seriously. Implement an anonymous reporting system so team members can report potential hazards discreetly. When employees know they can raise concerns without fear of retaliation, they're more likely to speak up, potentially preventing future incidents.

Know When to Involve Legal Support

A personal injury attorney can be an invaluable asset in shaping and maintaining a strong safety program. Consult your attorney when designing new policies or updating existing ones to ensure compliance with local and federal regulations. Their insight can help you avoid legal pitfalls and reduce liability exposure. If an incident does occur, having a long-standing relationship with an attorney means faster response times and better-informed decisions.

Taking action means more than putting rules on paper - it means building a dynamic, collaborative approach to safety that protects your people and your business. When combined with strong legal guidance and a culture of accountability, your safety plan becomes a foundation for long-term success.

FAQs

When should I consult a personal injury attorney for my business?

Seek legal counsel when introducing new safety protocols or encountering legal risks to ensure compliance and protect your business interests.

How can I minimize the risk of workplace accidents?

Conduct routine safety audits to identify and address potential hazards. Pair this with ongoing employee training to reinforce safe practices, improve awareness, and ensure compliance with evolving workplace standards.

What should I include in a workers' comp claim process?

Establish clear filing procedures for incidents, conduct thorough investigations to uncover root causes, and maintain prompt, transparent communication with employees to foster trust, accountability, and effective resolution of safety issues.

Bringing It All Together

Integrating a personal injury attorney into your business risk management strategy isn't just smart. It's essential. These legal professionals bring a critical layer of protection and guidance that helps you navigate the complex landscape of workplace safety and liability. By involving an attorney early in the process, you can identify potential legal vulnerabilities, craft compliant safety policies, and ensure that all preventative measures are in line with current laws and regulations.

Their role becomes even more crucial during an incident. From overseeing internal investigations to managing communication with injured parties, an attorney ensures your business responds effectively, lawfully, and with minimal disruption. Regular consultation allows you to stay ahead of legal changes, adapt to new risks, and foster a workplace culture centered around accountability and safety.

Ultimately, partnering with a personal injury attorney strengthens your overall risk management plan, reduces exposure to legal and financial fallout, and supports a more secure, resilient business.

Tips for Crafting a Personalized Financial Recovery Plan

Have you found yourself in a financial bind recently? Are you unsure how to bounce back and regain control over your finances? You're not alone.

Financial setbacks can be daunting, but with a well-crafted recovery plan tailored to your unique situation, you can get back on track. This guide is designed to help you navigate through the process of creating a personalized financial recovery plan.

We'll address common concerns and provide actionable tips to help you build a stable financial future. Ready to take the first step towards financial recovery?

Understanding Your Financial Situation

Before you can create a recovery plan, it's crucial to have a clear understanding of your current financial situation. Gather all your financial documents, including bank statements, credit card bills, loan statements, and any other relevant records. Take note of your income, expenses, debts, and assets.

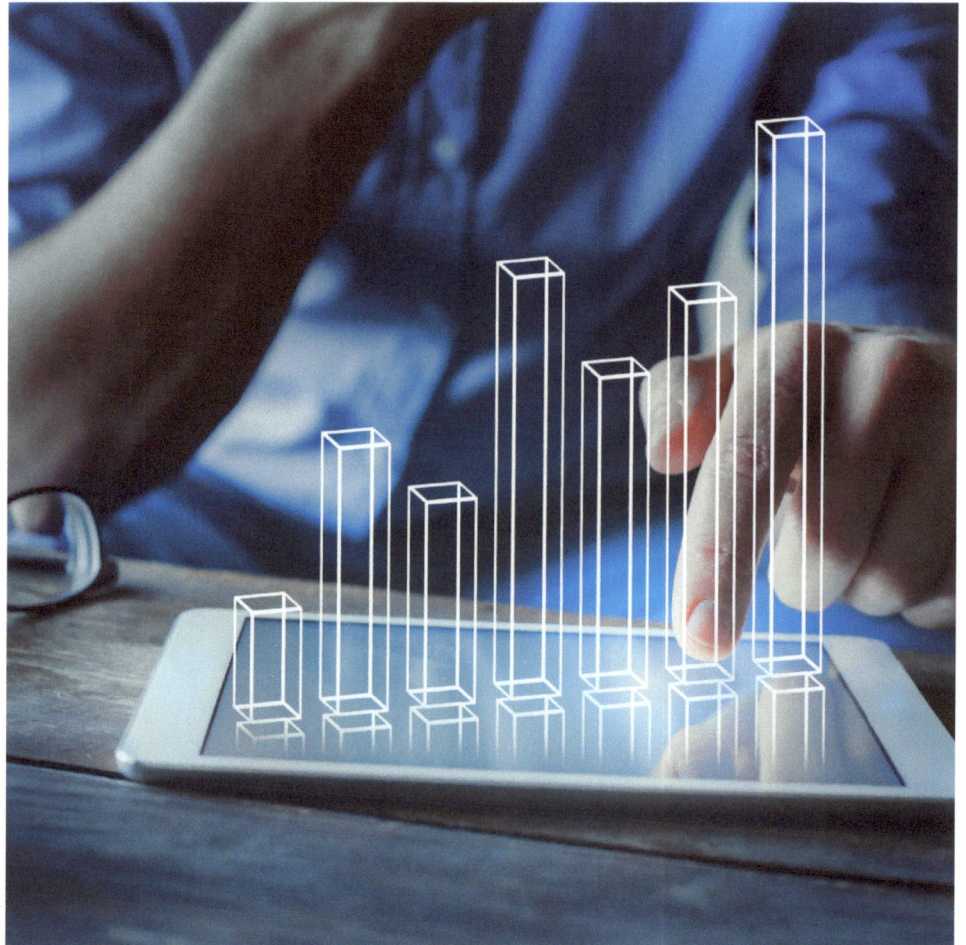

This evaluation will give you a comprehensive overview of where you stand financially. Identify the causes of your financial troubles, like overspending or lack of savings. This helps you avoid similar mistakes later. Set clear, achievable goals for recovery. Make short-term and long-term goals that are specific and measurable, like paying off debt or saving for a house.

Creating a Budget

Track Your Income and Expenses

Creating a budget is the cornerstone of any financial recovery plan. Start by tracking your income and expenses meticulously. Use budgeting apps or spreadsheets to record every source of income and every expenditure.

This practice will help you

understand your spending patterns and identify areas where you can cut back.

Categorize Your Expenses

Categorizing your expenses will provide a clearer picture of your spending habits. Divide your expenses into fixed and variable categories.

Fixed expenses include rent, utilities, and loan payments, while variable expenses encompass groceries, entertainment, and dining out. This categorization will help you prioritize essential expenses and identify discretionary spending that can be reduced.

Prioritize Essential Spending

When crafting your budget, prioritize essential spending over discretionary expenses. Focus on covering basic needs such as housing, utilities, food, and transportation. Allocate funds for debt repayments and savings before considering non-essential purchases.

This disciplined approach will ensure that your financial priorities are aligned with your recovery goals.

Managing Debt

Assess Your Debt Situation

A crucial aspect of financial recovery is managing and reducing your debt. Start by assessing your debt situation comprehensively. List all your debts, including credit card balances, personal loans, student loans, and any other outstanding obligations. Note the interest rates, minimum payments, and due dates for each debt.

In the U.S., debt settlement is a common strategy for dealing with significant debt. It involves negotiating with creditors to settle debts for less than the full amount owed, often leading to reduced payments or forgiving a portion of the debt. For many, understanding how debt settlement works can be crucial in making informed decisions.

For example, if you're located in Indiana, it's important to be aware of how debt settlement works in Indiana specifically. The state's regulations and practices can impact the effectiveness and options available for debt settlement. Recent statistics show that nearly 10% of Indiana residents face challenges severe enough to consider debt settlement as a viable solution. Exploring local resources and professional advice can provide valuable insights into the best approach for your situation.

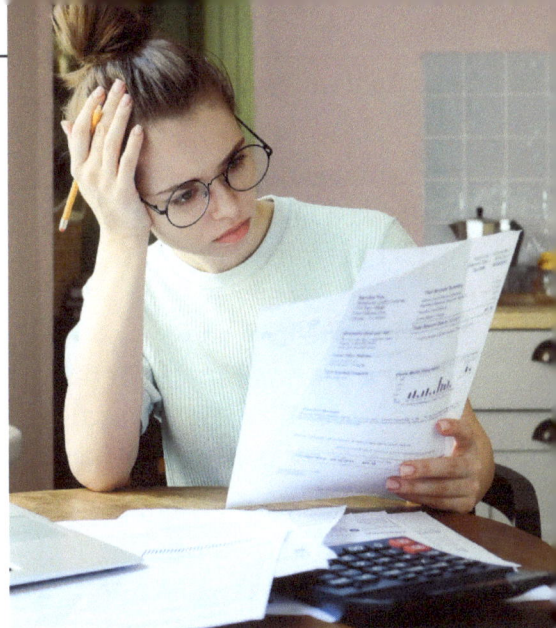

Develop a Debt Repayment Strategy

Once you have a clear picture of your debts, develop a repayment strategy. There are several methods you can use, including the debt avalanche and debt snowball methods. The debt avalanche method focuses on paying off high-interest debts first, while the debt snowball method targets the smallest debts first. Choose the method that aligns with your financial situation and preferences.

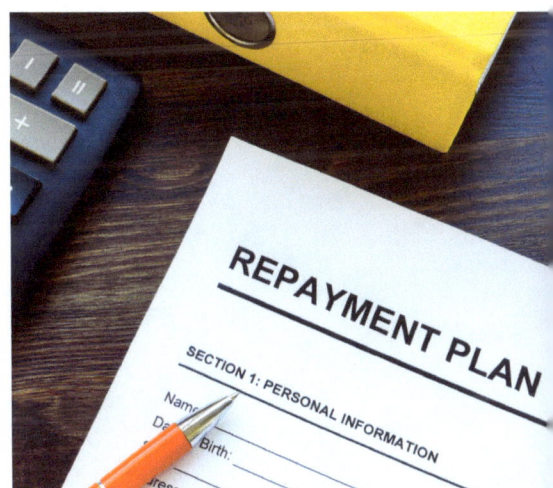

Debt Avalanche Method

The debt avalanche method involves paying off debts with the highest interest rates first. This strategy can save you money in the long run by reducing the amount of interest you pay over time. Here's a quick comparison of the two methods:

Debt Snowball Method: The debt snowball method focuses on paying off the smallest debts first, regardless of interest rates. This approach provides quick psychological wins, which can motivate you to continue your debt repayment journey.

Negotiate with Creditors: If you're struggling to make payments, consider negotiating with your creditors. Many creditors are willing to work with you to create a more manageable payment plan. Explain your situation honestly and request lower interest rates, reduced monthly payments, or temporary forbearance. Negotiating with creditors can provide much-needed relief and help you stay on track with your recovery plan.

Debt Repayment Strategies

Feature	Debt Avalanche Method	Debt Snowball Method
Focus	High-interest debts	Smallest debts
Psychological Benefit	Less immediate, more long-term savings	Immediate, small victories
Interest Savings	Higher overall savings due to less interest	Lower savings, but faster debt reduction feel
Time to First Victory	Longer due to larger debts being prioritized	Shorter due to quick payoff of small debts
Best For	Those with high-interest debt	Those needing quick motivation

Seek Professional Help

Sometimes managing debt can feel overwhelming. If you need assistance, consider seeking help from a credit counselor or financial advisor. These professionals can provide personalized advice and help you create a debt management plan.

Building an Emergency Fund

Importance of an Emergency Fund

An emergency fund is a critical component of financial stability. It provides a safety net for unexpected expenses, such as medical bills, car repairs, or job loss.

Having an emergency fund can prevent you from relying on credit cards or loans during emergencies, reducing the risk of falling into debt.

Determine Your Emergency Fund Goal

Determine the amount you need to save for your emergency fund. Financial experts recommend saving three to six months' worth of living expenses.

Calculate your essential monthly expenses and multiply that amount by the number of months you want to cover. Set this as your emergency fund goal.

Benefits of an Emergency Fund

1. Financial Security: Provides a cushion for unexpected expenses.

2. Debt Prevention: Reduces the need to borrow money during emergencies.

3. Peace of Mind: Offers psychological comfort knowing you have a financial backup.

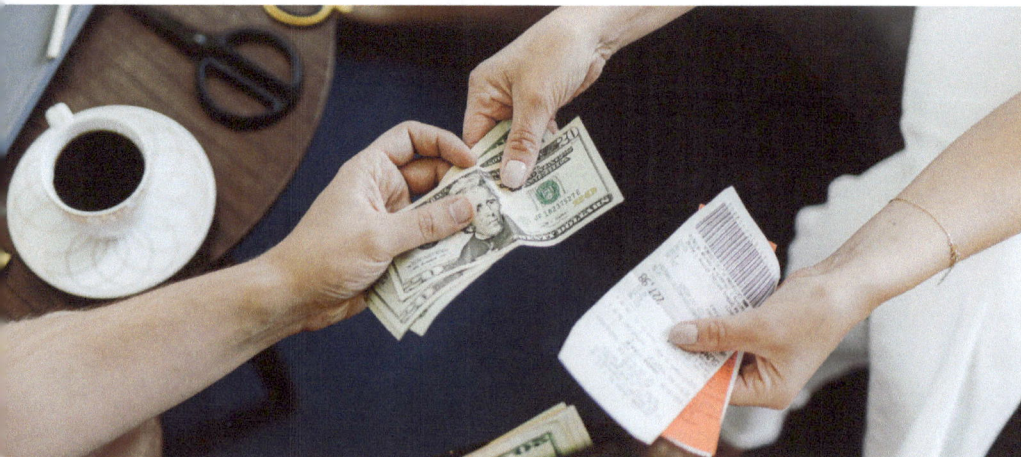

Start Small and Automate Savings

Building an emergency fund takes time, especially if you're already dealing with financial challenges. Start by saving small amounts regularly.

Automate your savings by setting up automatic transfers from your checking account to a dedicated savings account. Treat your emergency fund contribution as a non-negotiable monthly expense.

Increasing Your Income

Explore Additional Income Sources

Increasing your income can significantly expedite your financial recovery. Explore additional income sources, such as freelancing, part-time jobs, or side businesses.

Identify your skills and interests and look for opportunities that align with them. Additional income can help you pay off debt faster and build your savings.

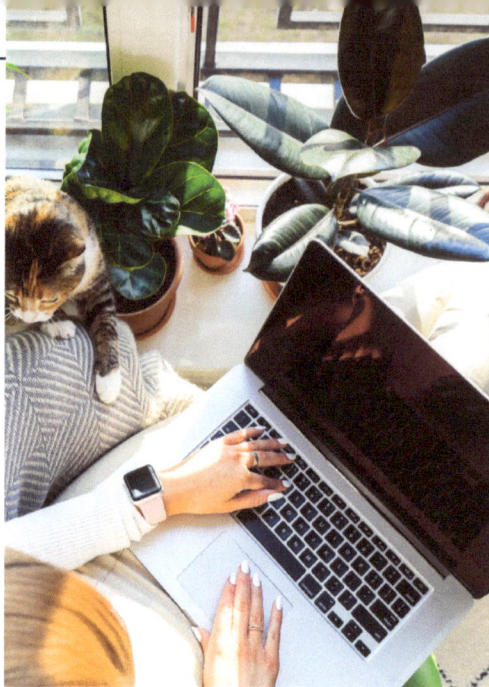

Freelancing Opportunities

- **Writing and Editing:** Websites, blogs, and magazines.

- **Graphic Design:** Logos, websites, marketing materials.

- **Tutoring:** Academic subjects, test preparation, language instruction.

Upskill and Invest in Education

Investing in your education and skills can enhance your earning potential. Consider taking courses or obtaining certifications that can boost your qualifications and make you more competitive in the job market. Upskilling can lead to higher-paying job opportunities and increased financial stability.

Negotiate Salary and Benefits

If you're currently employed, don't hesitate to negotiate your salary and benefits. Research industry standards and gather evidence of your contributions to the company.

Prepare a compelling case for why you deserve a raise or additional benefits. Effective negotiation can lead to a higher income, improving your financial situation.

Saving and Investing

Create a Savings Plan

Saving money is a fundamental aspect of financial recovery. Create a savings plan that aligns with your financial goals. Set aside a portion of your income for short-term and long-term savings.

Short-term savings can be used for upcoming expenses, while long-term savings can be directed towards retirement or major financial goals.

Explore Investment Options

Investing can help grow your wealth and provide additional income streams. Educate

INVESTMENT

yourself about different investment options, such as stocks, bonds, mutual funds, and real estate. Diversify your investments to minimize risk and maximize returns. Consider consulting a financial advisor to develop an investment strategy that suits your risk tolerance and financial goals.

Monitor and Adjust Your Portfolio

Regularly monitor your investment portfolio to ensure it aligns with your financial objectives. Market conditions and personal circumstances can change, so it's important to review and adjust your investments periodically. Rebalancing your portfolio can help maintain the right mix of assets and optimize your returns.

Building Financial Discipline

Building financial discipline requires mindful spending. Before making a purchase, ask yourself if it's a necessity or a want. Consider the long-term impact of your spending decisions on your financial recovery.

Practicing mindful spending will help you make intentional choices and avoid impulsive purchases. As your financial situation improves, it's essential to avoid lifestyle inflation. Lifestyle inflation occurs when your spending increases proportionally with your income. Instead of upgrading your lifestyle, focus on saving and investing the additional income.

Live modestly to recover faster and reach goals sooner. Set milestones to stay motivated and on track. Break them down into smaller steps, celebrate progress, and stay focused on your goals.

Utilizing Financial Tools and Resources

Leveraging financial tools and resources can streamline your recovery process. Budgeting apps and software can help you track your income, expenses, and savings goals. Popular options include Mint, YNAB (You Need a Budget), and Personal Capital. These tools provide real-time insights into your financial health and assist in making informed decisions.

Monitor your credit score regularly to catch potential issues early. Use free services like Credit Karma, Experian, and TransUnion to get alerts for suspicious activity. Learn about personal finance through books, blogs, podcasts, and online courses. Stay informed to make better financial decisions.

Seeking Professional Help

Financial Advisors and Planners

If you're struggling to create an effective financial recovery plan, consider seeking help from a financial advisor or planner. These professionals can provide personalized guidance based on your unique financial situation. They can help you develop a comprehensive plan, optimize your investments, and navigate complex financial decisions.

Credit Counseling Services

Credit counseling services can assist you in managing your debt and improving your credit.

Nonprofit organizations like the National Foundation for Credit Counseling (NFCC) offer free or low-cost credit counseling. Credit counselors can negotiate with creditors on your behalf, create a debt management plan, and provide financial education to help you stay on track.

Legal and Tax Professionals

In some cases, legal and tax issues may complicate your financial recovery. Consulting with legal and tax professionals can help you address these challenges effectively. They can provide advice on bankruptcy, tax resolution, estate planning, and other complex matters. Seeking professional assistance ensures that you make informed decisions and comply with legal requirements.

Maintaining Long-Term Financial Health

- **Regularly Review Your Financial Plan:** Regularly review your financial plan, assess progress, and make changes as needed. Adapt to evolving life circumstances and goals to ensure long-term financial health.

- **Continue Educating Yourself:** Learn about personal finance, investments, and economic trends. Stay updated through newsletters, workshops, and online communities.

- **Stay Positive and Persistent:** Stay positive and focused to overcome financial setbacks. Celebrate small wins and surround yourself with supportive people. With determination, you can build a secure financial future.

Frequently Asked Questions

1. What should I do first to start my financial recovery?

Begin by evaluating your current financial status. Gather all financial documents and create a detailed list of your income, expenses, debts, and assets.

2. How can I effectively create and stick to a budget?

Track all your income and expenses, categorize them, and prioritize essential spending. Use budgeting apps to help you stay on track.

3. What are some strategies to manage and reduce my debt?

Consider using debt repayment methods like the debt avalanche or debt snowball. Negotiating with creditors for better terms can also be beneficial.

4. How important is having an emergency fund, and how much should I save?

An emergency fund is crucial for financial stability. Aim to save three to six months' worth of living expenses to cover unexpected costs.

5. Can a professional help make a difference in my financial recovery plan?

Yes, consulting financial advisors, credit counselors, or legal and tax professionals can provide personalized guidance and help you make informed decisions.

Key Takeaways

- Understand your current financial situation by listing all income, expenses, debts, and assets.

- Define short-term and long-term financial goals that are SMART (Specific, Measurable, Achievable, Relevant, and Time-bound).

- Track income and expenses, prioritize essential spending, and use budgeting tools for better management.

- Use debt repayment strategies like the debt avalanche or snowball method and consider negotiating with creditors.

- Practice mindful spending, avoid lifestyle inflation, and set up financial milestones to stay motivated.

Taking control of your financial future starts with a single step - committing to change. While creating a personalized financial recovery plan may feel overwhelming, it's completely within reach with a thoughtful, structured approach. Begin by taking an honest look at your current financial situation, identifying both challenges and opportunities. Set clear, achievable goals that align with your lifestyle and values. A well-crafted budget becomes your blueprint, guiding your spending and helping you make smarter decisions. Managing debt is crucial - prioritize high-interest balances and consider consolidation or repayment strategies that ease the burden. Most importantly, cultivate financial discipline by tracking progress, avoiding impulsive spending, and celebrating small wins along the way.

Financial recovery doesn't happen overnight. It's a process that requires patience, consistency, and self-awareness. But with the right mindset and a proactive plan, you can transform your finances and regain confidence in your future. The journey starts when you decide you're ready.

The Future of E-Commerce: Trends to Watch in the Next Decade

E-commerce isn't just evolving. It's undergoing a full-blown reinvention. What once began as a simple online checkout system has now exploded into a sophisticated, data-powered ecosystem that influences everything from logistics to customer experience. The old model of clicking and shipping has been replaced by real-time personalization, AI-driven engagement, and immersive digital journeys that blur the line between physical and virtual retail.

Consumer expectations are rising fast. They want speed, relevance, transparency and they want it across every device, platform, and touchpoint. Meanwhile, technologies like AI, augmented reality, and blockchain aren't just supporting e-commerce - they're redefining it. Brands are no longer just competing on price or product. They're competing on experience, trust, and agility.

So what's next?

The next decade of e-commerce will be shaped by five pivotal forces: hyper-personalization, immersive shopping experiences, social commerce, mobile-first behavior, and the rise of blockchain-powered infrastructure. These aren't passing trends. They're fundamental shifts in how commerce will function in the digital world. For business leaders, staying ahead of these changes isn't a nice-to-have. It's mission-critical.

Let's dive into these powerful shifts and explore how forward-thinking businesses can adapt, innovate, and thrive in a landscape where change is the only constant.

1. Mobile Commerce: Where Every Click Counts

The days of optimizing for desktop are long gone. Mobile is no longer "part" of the customer journey. It is the journey. Mobile commerce (m-commerce) has

FOR EVERY BUSINESS & BUDGET

Looking for a website design firm or D.I.Y. platform that can help you build a visually stunning and effective online brand? Look no further than our expert team. At Proshark, we help you build a customized website that meets your unique needs and goals and converts visitors to customers.

PROSHARK SITES

INNOVATION DESIGNED TO INSPIRE

www.proshark.com

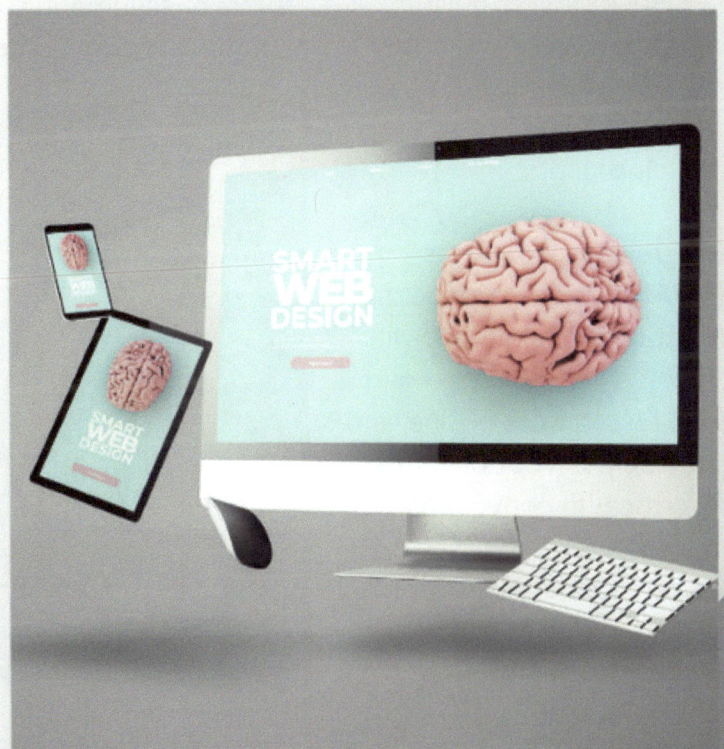

taken center stage, and its influence is only growing.

Why it matters:

According to Statista, mobile commerce sales are expected to account for nearly 75% of total e-commerce by 2028.

As screen time increases and shopping behaviors become more impulsive and convenience-driven, businesses that ignore mobile optimization will fall behind fast.

Key developments:

- **Progressive Web Apps (PWAs):** These combine the functionality of an app with the reach of the web. PWAs load faster, work offline, and provide push notifications - all critical to conversion.

- **Voice commerce:** Smart speakers and mobile assistants are powering voice-based shopping. Expect a rise in purchases triggered by simple verbal commands.

- **Mobile-first content design:** Short-form video, vertical product images, and tap-friendly UI are critical for mobile-native users—especially Gen Z.

What to do:

- Audit your entire purchase journey on mobile.

- Optimize product pages for speed and clarity.

- Test mobile-exclusive offers and loyalty programs.

The brands dominating mobile commerce are designing seamless, intuitive experiences that anticipate user behavior turning everyday scrolls into frictionless micro-moments that drive engagement, trust, and immediate conversions.

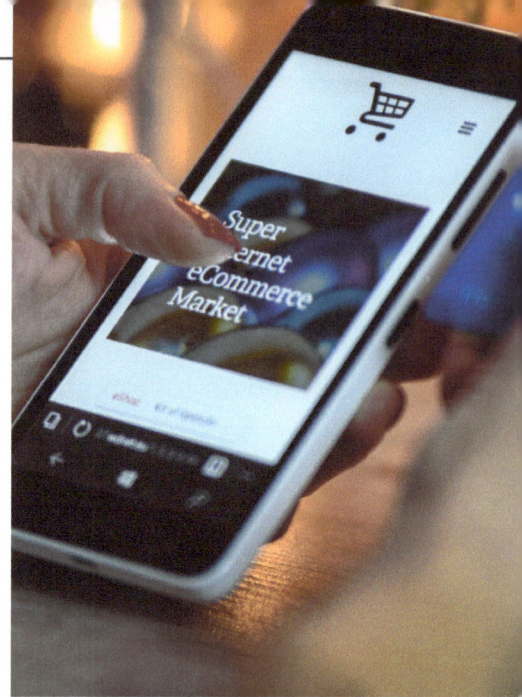

2. Hyper-Personalization: The Data Gold Rush

Generic messaging is a relic of the past. Customers want tailored experiences that speak to their lifestyle, preferences, and values in real time.

Where it's heading:

Hyper-personalization is powered by AI and real-time data analytics. It moves beyond simply showing "related items" and into dynamic, behavioral targeting. Think Netflix-style recommendation engines but for skincare, supplements, or apparel.

Emerging tools:

- **Predictive AI:** Algorithms that anticipate what customers want before they ask.

- **Zero-party data strategies:** Brands are now asking customers directly for preferences, style choices, and values then tailoring based on that feedback.

- **Behavior-triggered automation:** Emails, texts, and push notifications that change based on customer actions or inactions.

Real-world example:

Brands like Stitch Fix and Function of Beauty are thriving on this model. They've built scalable personalization into their product development and marketing engines and customers love it.

Action step:

Start small with tailored email flows and product suggestions. Then build toward integrating AI that personalizes the homepage, search results, and promotional offers based on user behavior.

In the next wave of e-commerce, personalization isn't a feature. It's the foundation.

3. Immersive Commerce: Try Before You Buy, Digitally

With rising competition and endless options, shoppers demand certainty before buying. Augmented Reality, Virtual Reality, and 3D commerce deliver immersive, hands-on previews that build trust and reduce hesitation at checkout.

Why it's big:

Visualizing a product in your space, on your face, or with your outfit reduces friction and returns. AR/VR bridges the trust gap between physical and digital.

What's trending:

- **Virtual try-ons:** Eyewear, makeup, apparel, and even shoes.

- **3D product views:** Users can spin, zoom, and interact with products in ways that 2D images can't deliver.

- **Virtual showrooms:** Forward-thinking brands are building entire virtual storefronts complete with virtual shopping assistants.

Tech that's leading:

- Shopify and BigCommerce are investing in native AR integrations.

- Tools like Wanna Kicks, ModiFace, and Roomvo are making immersive tech accessible to small brands.

Next-level innovation:

Haptic feedback is on the horizon. Soon, users may be able to "feel" a texture through wearable tech or simulate product handling with smart gloves.

Immersive commerce isn't just about being flashy. It's about reducing buyer hesitation and boosting satisfaction.

4. Social Commerce: Where Discovery Meets Checkout

Social media has matured from a marketing tool to a commerce engine. Gen Z and Millennials are skipping Google search entirely and turning to TikTok, Instagram, and YouTube to discover what to buy.

What's happening:

- **Shoppable video is exploding:** TikTok Shop and Instagram Reels now allow users to go from inspiration to checkout in seconds.

- **Live commerce:** Live product demos, Q&As, and exclusive drops are driving urgency and conversions in real-time.

- **Creator-led shopping:** Influencers aren't just promoting products. They're curating entire storefronts.

The trust factor:

Consumers trust people over brands. That's why user-generated content (UGC), unboxing videos, and real customer reviews drive more conversions than polished brand ads.

Platform spotlight:

- **TikTok Shop:** A massive success in Southeast Asia and now growing in the U.S., it merges entertainment and impulse buying.

- **Pinterest Shopping:** A visual-first discovery engine that's quietly evolving into a powerful sales channel.

How to win:

- Partner with niche creators who truly use your product.

- Build out shoppable experiences that feel native to the platform.

- Repurpose top-performing organic content into paid campaigns.

Social commerce isn't the future - it's the present. If you're not selling where your customers scroll, you're already losing them.

5. Blockchain and Decentralized Commerce: The Quiet Revolution

While most e-commerce trends are visible to the consumer, blockchain is working behind the scenes to build a more secure, transparent, and frictionless future.

Use cases gaining traction:

- **Provenance & traceability:** Shoppers want to know where products come from. Blockchain lets them verify every step—from raw materials to final delivery.

- **Smart contracts:** These self-executing agreements can handle order fulfillment, payments, refunds, and even loyalty perks without a middleman.

- **Decentralized marketplaces:** Platforms like Origin Protocol are testing what commerce looks like without tech giants taking a cut.

Payment revolution:

Blockchain also powers faster, cheaper global transactions through cryptocurrencies and stablecoins. Expect adoption to rise, especially in regions with volatile banking systems.

Who's experimenting:

Luxury brands like LVMH are using blockchain to verify authenticity. Food brands are tracking ethical sourcing. Some Shopify merchants are already accepting crypto.

Potential roadblocks:

Mass adoption still faces challenges, mainly education, regulation, and usability. But the momentum is undeniable.

As Web3 evolves, blockchain could become the invisible infrastructure supporting next-gen commerce just like cloud computing did in the 2010s.

Bonus Trend: Conscious Commerce and Sustainable Operations

Consumers are holding brands to higher standards and rewarding the ones that deliver. From eco-friendly packaging to transparent labor practices, sustainability is becoming a purchase driver, not just a talking point.

How it shows up:

- Carbon tracking at checkout

- Circular commerce models (resale, rentals, refills)

- Transparent impact reporting

Tools to explore:

Tools like EcoCart, Shopify Planet, and GreenStory empower brands to integrate carbon offsets, eco-impact data, and responsible practices directly into the checkout experience turning sustainability into a seamless customer touchpoint.

What This All Means for You

The next decade of e-commerce won't reward those who chase every shiny trend. It will favor brands that stay adaptable, data-driven, and deeply human in their approach. Flexibility means being able to pivot quickly as technologies evolve and consumer behaviors shift. Being data-smart means using insights to guide meaningful decisions, not just fuel vanity metrics. And human-centricity? That's the heart of it all. Building experiences that feel personal, intuitive, and trustworthy. Businesses that succeed will be the ones that listen more, personalize better, and move faster without losing the human touch. In a digital world, relevance comes from real connection and agility.

The winners in this space will:

- Prioritize mobile experiences that feel native, fast, and functional.

- Use data not just to sell more, but to serve better.

- Create immersive experiences that build trust.

- Meet customers where they are especially on social.

- Lay the groundwork for future-proof systems like blockchain and AI.

E-COMMERCE

We're entering a pivotal era in e-commerce - one where success is no longer built on convenience alone. The next generation of online commerce is about forging meaningful connections with customers, offering clarity in every transaction, and bringing creativity into the shopping experience. As the digital marketplace becomes more saturated, standing out will depend on how well a business understands and adapts to its audience. It's not about having the largest budget or the biggest warehouse. It's about delivering relevance, trust, and innovation at every touchpoint.

Consumers are more informed, empowered, and selective than ever. They expect seamless mobile experiences, personalized journeys, ethical choices, and immersive storytelling that goes beyond products. Brands that meet these expectations with transparency, speed, and a human touch will thrive in this evolving landscape.

Whether you're launching your first online store or steering a legacy brand through digital transformation, the same principle applies: agility beats size. The most adaptable businesses, those willing to evolve with technology, customer behavior, and market dynamics, will shape the future of commerce.
This isn't just a shift in tools; it's a shift in mindset. And those ready to lead with purpose and flexibility will redefine what success looks like in the digital economy.

www.ingramcontent.com/pod-product-compliance
Lightning Source LLC
Chambersburg PA
CBHW041703200326
41518CB00002B/175